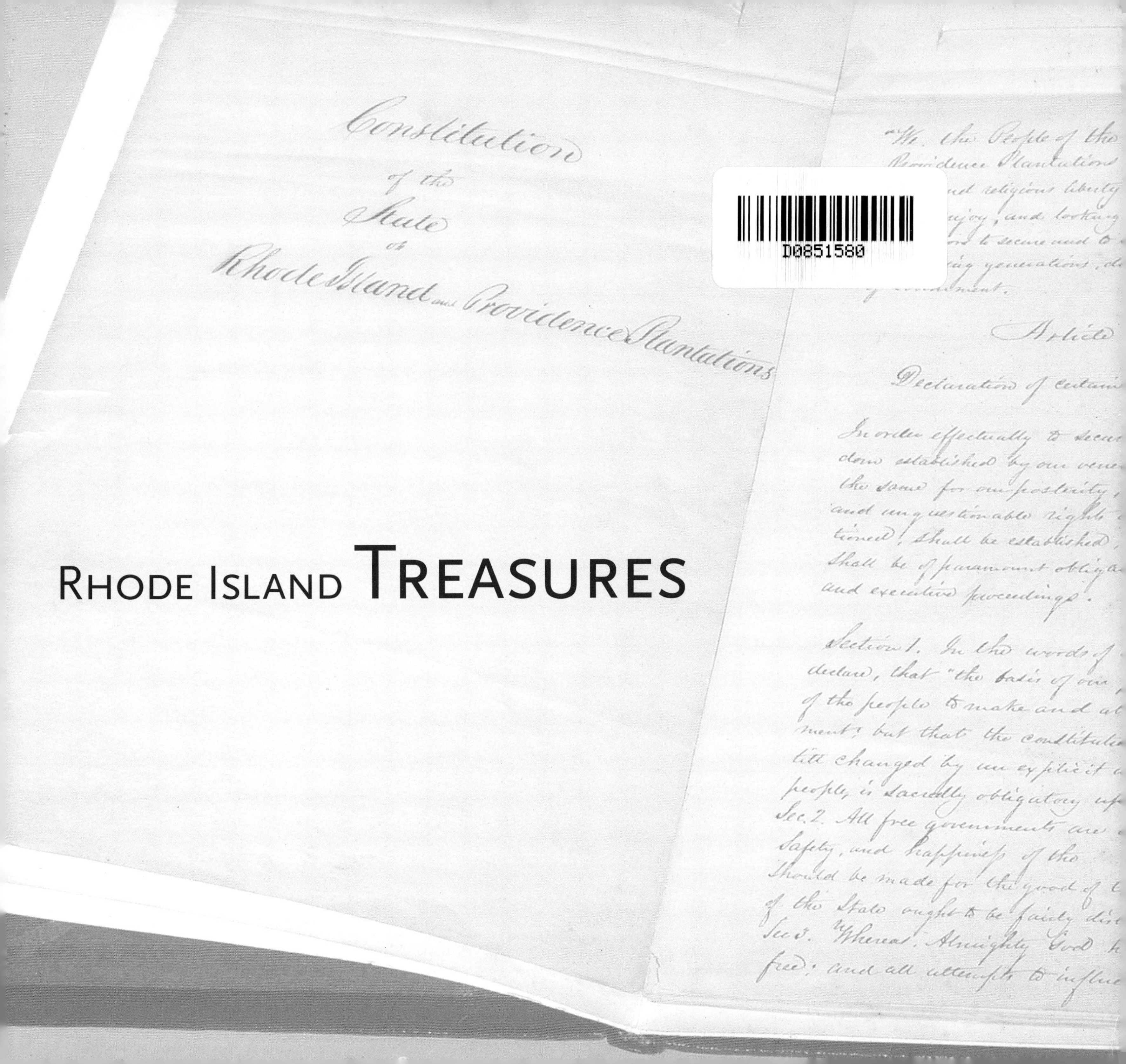

Rhode Island Treasures

This book was edited by JAMES WILSON and printed by NARRAGANSETT GRAPHICS in Coventry, Rhode Island. It is printed on 100 LB. Corniche Velvet Text.

The book was designed and typeset by GAIL SOLOMON of Providence, Rhode Island. The main text is set in *Adobe Garamond* and *Adobe Garamond "Expert"* with oldstyle figures. Supplemental type is set in *Scala Sans*.

Digital photographs were taken at Touro Synagogue, The Newport Historical Society, The Preservation Society of Newport County, The Varnum Memorial Armory, The Providence Jewelry Museum, Slater Mill, The South County Museum, The Museum of Natural History at Roger Williams Park, The Rhode Island State Archives and Warwick City Hall by BEAU JONES, IMAGES DESIGN COMPANY of Wakefield, Rhode Island.

The photo on the front cover was recently discovered in the attic of Providence City Hall. No one knows the names of the young men, or exactly when the picture was taken. Its mysterious nature fuels our fascination. For us, it symbolizes all the people of Rhode Island, full of hope, who have worked so hard — often with little recognition — to keep our spirit alive. These young men, whoever they were, truly are *Rhode Island Treasures.*

Contents

Roger Williams' compass, page 5

A Driving Spirit...

STRUGGLE

Battle of Rhode Island, page 12

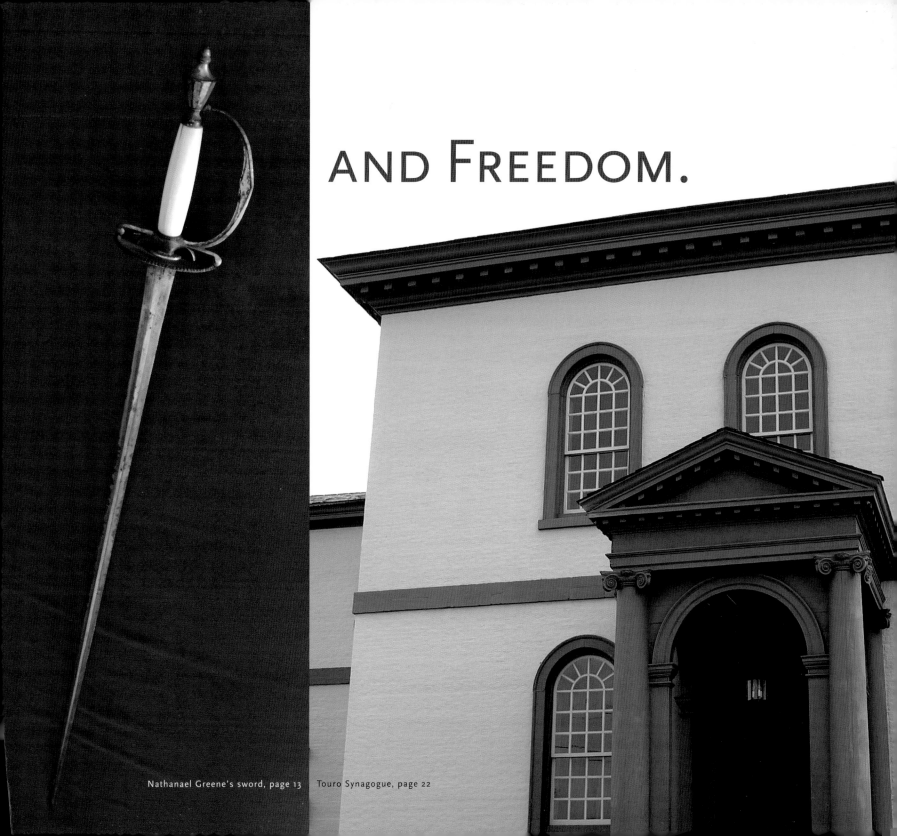

AND FREEDOM.

Nathanael Greene's sword, page 13   Touro Synagogue, page 22

THE GRAND

water wheel at Slater Mill, page 43

ART,

AND THE HUMBLE.

jewelry industry: 1947 advertisement and findings board, page 48

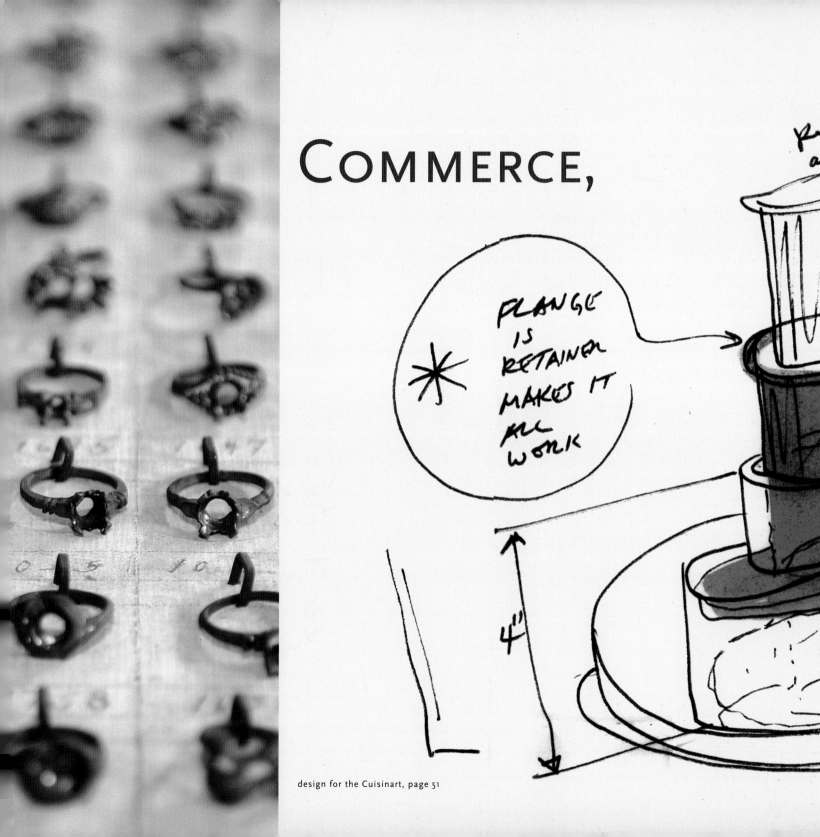

COMMERCE,

FLANGE IS RETAINER MAKES IT ALL WORK

Pusher area

FOOD

4"

AND INGENUITY.

RHODE ISLAND TREASURES

RHODE ISLAND TREASURES is a celebration of the people of America's smallest state. Early in our history, Rhode Island distinguished itself as one of the most creative and dynamic contributors of what defines the American spirit and character. Economically, culturally, socially, artistically, and spiritually, Rhode Island represents the best of what it means to be American. The people of Rhode Island have always been characterized as tough, fearless, innovative, and above all, faithful to our country's fundamental belief in the value of individual liberty.

From its earliest days, Rhode Island has shown courage and inventiveness. For example, during the Revolutionary War when the British invaded Aquidneck Island, Rhode Island created a strategic alliance with the French and ultimately became the first state to achieve its independence from Britain. In the 17th century, Roger Williams literally changed the world when he established Rhode Island as a sanctuary for religious freedom. Also Matilda Sissieretta Joyner Jones, a black woman in the late 19th century, became one of the most renowned opera singers of her time. Being the smallest state has never inhibited the people of Rhode Island. We have always known how to survive and flourish in spite of seemingly impossible odds, and we make a habit of passing that quality on to our children and our children's children.

Rhode Island has always known that its greatest treasure is its people and has always trusted in the fundamental talents, creativity, and decency of its citizenry to carry it through to success. What sets Rhode Island apart is its astonishing diversity — and its abiding unity as a community of caring people. *Rhode Island Treasures* is a celebration of these remarkable people of Rhode Island. You will never think of Rhode Island as small again.

The first Rhode Island colonial flag, on loan from the Redwood Library and Athenaeum.

INDEPENDENT SPIRIT

Land deed between Roger Williams and the Native Americans loaned by Providence City Hall.

Native American Clay Pottery

Newly found early Native American pottery proves that people were settled in year-round villages in New England as early as 500 BC. The discovery of pointed pots on Block Island was the first clue that civilization on the that site pre-dated agriculture. Since pointed pots were placed into a fire and rounded pots were suspended above the fire, a conclusion was drawn that pointed pots are from a much earlier time period than rounded ones. These pots were given radiocarbon dating tests. The results showed that the pots were between 2,350 and 2,550 years old, pushing back the estimated date of year-round settlements in New England and proving that permanent settlements were possible without agriculture.

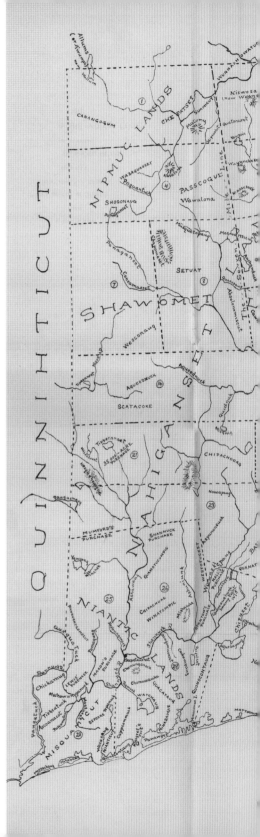

Native American clay pot on loan from Rhode Island College.

MAP OF THE
COLONY OF RHODE ISLAND
giving the
INDIAN NAMES OF LOCATIONS
THE LOCATIONS OF GREAT EVENTS IN INDIAN HISTORY
with
Present Political Divisions Indicated
by
SIDNEY S. RIDER
Providence Rhode Island 1903

ing to Act of Congress in the year 1903 by Sidney S. Rider in the Office
of the Librarian of Congress at Washington

Map with Native American Names

The names of many places in Rhode Island originated with the Native American tribes who inhabited them. Places such as Quonset, Matunuck, Narragansett, Scituate, Aquidneck, Chepachet, Pawtucket, and Weybosset have held onto their native names. Even as white settlers enveloped their lands, the Native American names held, forever reminding us of their heritage and culture.

Roger Williams' Compass and Sundial

Banished from Puritan Massachusetts, Roger Williams fled southward through the wilderness to the shores of Narragansett Bay. He named his new home *Providence* in gratitude "for God's merciful providence unto me in my distress," and there his "new and dangerous opinions" about religious liberty flourished.

It has long been believed that this 17th-century sundial/compass, given to the Rhode Island Historical Society by a descendant in 1902, guided Roger Williams on his journey. This famous relic has come to symbolize the Ocean State's origins as an experiment in tolerance. Apparently unmodified except for the probable modern replacement of the fragile wooden needle, the sundial/compass survives in almost perfect condition.

Map image from the Heritage Harbor Museum. Compass and sundial loaned by the Rhode Island Historical Society.

Land Deed Between Native Americans and Roger Williams

Unlike other settlers, Roger Williams felt little fear of the Native Americans who were his neighbors. He spent much time with them, learning their language and securing friendly relationships. One of his closest companions was the Indian sachem, Canonicus. When Williams and his followers landed on the shores of Canonicus' territory after fleeing the Massachusetts Bay Colony, they were well received. Within the year Roger Williams began negotiations with the natives to legally obtain land from them, recognizing the rights of those who resided there. He obtained the a land deed initially as a verbal agreement and then in the form of a "memorandum." It was signed first by Canonicus who marked his signature with the mark of an Indian canoe, and then by the sachem Miantonomi who made his mark with the sketch of an arrow.

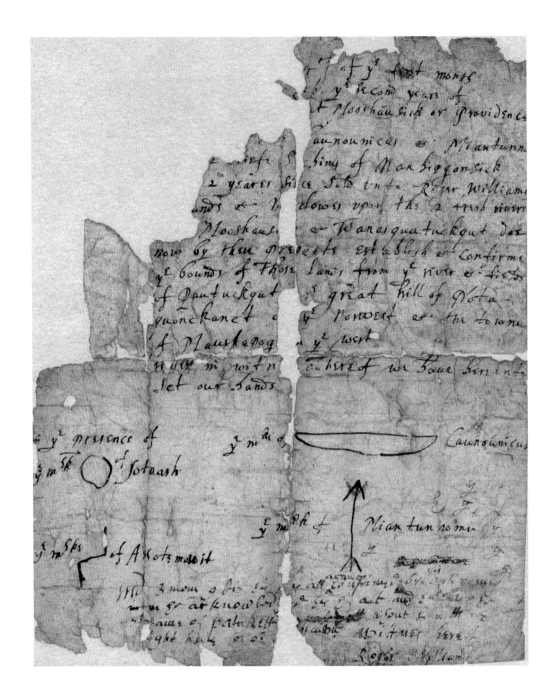

Land deed between Roger Williams and the Native Americans loaned by Providence City Hall.

Roger Williams' Bible by John Eliot

17th-century Puritans made a variety of attempts to convert the local Native American populations to Christianity. John Eliot is perhaps the best known of the Protestant missionaries to the Native Americans, beginning in the early 1640's.

Eliot, a minister in Roxbury, Massachusetts, translated the Old and New Testaments into the Algonquin language. The New Testament was published in 1661, and the Old Testament in 1663. It was the first bible to be published in America in any language. Roger Williams owned this copy of the 1663 first edition of John Eliot's *Indian Bible*. The *Indian Bible* is without question the rarest and most historically significant book in the colonial College Library of Brown University.

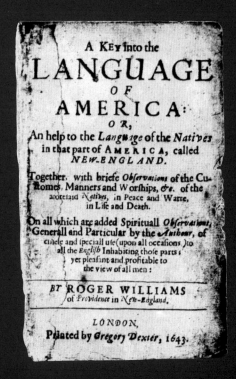

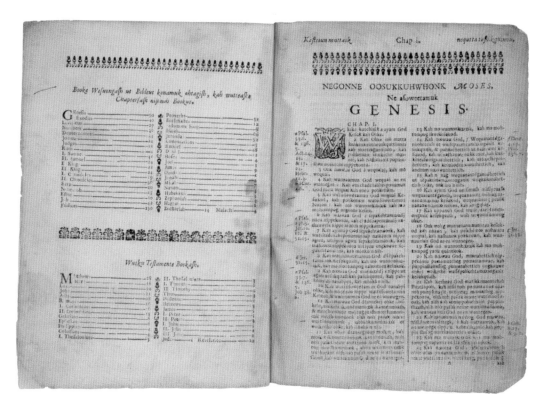

The Eliot Bible and *A Key Into the Language of America* are on loan from the John Hay Library, Brown University.

A Key Into the Language of America

In 1643 Roger Williams published some of his sympathetic observations of the Native American people in his book, *A Key Into the Language of America*. This book is the first extensive vocabulary and analysis of a Native American language printed in English. It also contains stories and observations about Native American life and culture. Williams wrote it to help his fellow colonists interact peacefully with their native neighbors.

Whereas By vertue of A free and absolute Charter of ciuill Incorporation Granted to the free Inhabitants of this Colony or province by the Right honorables Robert Earle of Warwicke gouerner in Chief with the rest of the honourable Comisioner Bearinge Date the fourteenth day of March in the Yeare one thousand Six Hundreth forty three and granting full power and Authoritie vnto the Said inhabitants to governe themselues and such other as Shall Come amonge them As also to make constitute and ordeyne such lawes orders and constitution and to inflict Such punishments and pennalties as is conformable to the lawes of England so neare or the and constitution of this place will admitt and which may Best Sute the estate and Condition therof And whereas the said Townes of providence ports mouth Newport and warwick are fare Remote each from other and free intercours of help in deciding of differences and trying of causes and the like cannot easily be had and procured as in this kind of requisett Therfore and upon the petition and Humbls Request of Towne of Warwick exhibited vnto this present Sessions of generall Assembly wherin by to incorporate themselues into a Body poilitike etc. Wee the said assembly hauing Duly weighed and seriously ad the premises and Being willing and Ready to provide for the ease and libertie of the people Haue thought Authoritie aforesaid And by these presents Do giue grant Ensigne and confirme this present C Said inhabitants of the Towne of Warwick All wing ordering and hereby Authorizing the part of them from time to time to Transeact all such Towne affaires as shall fale within the and presincts of the said Towne As also to make and constitute such perticuler orders penalltles and may Best Suit with the Condition of the said Towne any Townshipp for the well bracing and governing therof provided the said Lawes constitutions and punishments flor the Ciuill Government therof bee able to the Lawes of England So farr as the Nature and Constitution of that Towne will Admitt and to theend wee do authorize them to Erect A Court of Justice and do giue them powre to execute such orders and penalties and so many of the Comon Lawes Agreed in the generall and their penalties as are not allready the generall Court of Tryalls And If further wee do Hearby Order the said Towne to Elect And ingage all Such officers as shalbe for the propagation of Justice and Judgment therin vpon the first munday In the month of Iune annually for ever hereafter Shall maintaine them in fidelitie to the Utmost of their powre The liberties and freedom of this Collonie And the priviledges of the Towne wherin they beare office and further Wee Do herby invest and Authorize the said officer So Elected and ingaged with full power to Transeact in the premyses and in so Deinge shall be Hearby Secured and Indemnified ——

Giuen at portsmouth at the generall Assembly there held this 14th of March Anno 1648 John Warner clerk of y assembly

Warwick Royal Charter, 1648

Banished for their beliefs, Samuel Gorton and his followers left Massachusetts to settle in Rhode Island, a colony known as a haven for the disaffected. However, Massachusetts claimed to have hold over the land known as Shawomet, where Gorton had intended to settle. Upset by the injustices inflicted upon him and his "Gortonists," Samuel Gorton sailed to England. He presented his case to Parliament and the lands of Shawomet were restored to him, much to the credit of Robert Rich, the earl of Warwick and governor-in-chief of foreign plantations.

Gorton returned to the colonies with full power over his reclaimed lands. He renamed Shawomet as Warwick in appreciation of the earl who had supported him in Parliament. A new government was established when Warwick was included in the charter for Rhode Island and Providence Plantations in March of 1647.

The First Rhode Island Colonial Flag

When Rhode Island was confirmed as a colony in 1663, King Charles II gave the colony its charter. Tradition holds that when the royal charter was given to the colony, the Rhode Island Colonial Magistrate met the British ship as it came into the Newport harbor bearing the Rhode Island Colonial flag. The flag was made from dyed blue cotton and painted with red crosses of St. Andrew and St. George.

This original flag was discovered in the 1850's when renovations were being made to the attic of the house of former Governor John Wanton. Wanton had served as governor of Rhode Island from 1734 to 1740 and had died in 1742. The 26" x 37" British "Union Jack" flag was most likely passed down through his family as they assumed roles in the colony's history.

The Royal Charter flag is on loan from the Redwood Library and Athenaeum.

The Gaspee Commission

The destruction of the British armed schooner *Gaspee*, off Namquid Point (now known as "Gaspee Point") in the "Narragansett River" was considered the first armed conflict leading to the American Revolution.

This document, the Gaspee Commission, initiated the Crown's investigation into the burning of the *Gaspee*, appointing commissioners who were to report an "account of all the circumstances relative to the attacking, taking and plundering and burning our said schooner." The orders by the King were addressed to the Joseph Wanton (Governor of the Rhode Island), James Horsemander (Chief Justice of New York), Frederick Smythe (Chief Justice of New Jersey), Peter Oliver (Chief Justice of Massachusetts Bay), and Robert Auchmuty (Judge of the Vice Admiralty Court in Boston). This commission was granted full power and authority to administer oaths, make indictments, investigate the causes of the rebellion, and to relay to the King a full and true account of the proceedings. Even though rewards were offered, no one ever spoke a word; no one became an informer.

The document is inscribed on vellum with a Royal Seal, and dated 2 September 1772.

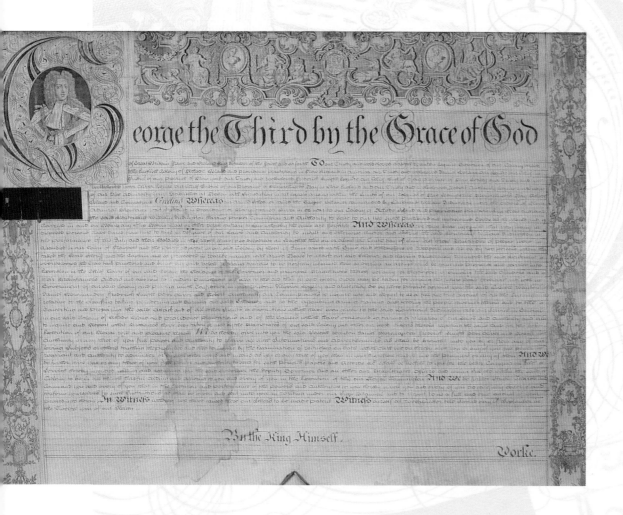

Revolutionary War Leather Helmet

The Battle of Long Island took place on August 27, 1776. In the early morning hours, the Americans were attacked by between 200 and 300 British troops. By the battle's end there were an estimated 10,000 American troops involved. It was estimated that 1,407 Americans were wounded, captured, or missing, and 312 killed. A British report said that there were 89 American officers imprisoned, and 1,097 other Americans also kept as prisoners. Based upon possession of the disputed territory and casualties sustained, the British had won this battle.

One American who lost his life in the Battle of Long Island was Captain Lieutenant Benajah Carpentier of Rhode Island. A member of the artillery division, he wore a leather helmet into battle which carried the motto, "For Our Country."

Revolutionary War Backpack

The Kentish Guards, a militia company chartered on October 29, 1774, used this backpack in the Revolutionary War and in the War of 1812. Though they were Patriots, the Kentish Guards (from Kent County) as well as other Rhode Island militia thought the best uniform would be red, based on the British model. Thus the backpack was painted red to match their uniforms.

The Kentish Guards were so well trained, equipped and disciplined that General Washington commissioned thirty-five of them as officers in the Continental Army after seeing them at the Siege of Boston in 1775.

This backpack was present at seven Rhode Island battles and at the birth of the United States Army and Navy.

The Revolutionary War leather helmet is on loan from the Varnum Armory. The Revolutionary War backpack has been loaned by the Kentish Guards, Rhode Island Militia.

Battle of Rhode Island
Aquidneck Island, 1778

Rhode Islanders witnessed one battle on their soil during the Revolutionary War. It took place at Butts Fort in Portsmouth on August 29, 1778. Here, the British foiled an attempt by the Americans to drive them from Aquidneck Island, which they had held for nearly three years.

Sir Henry Clinton and Major Howe led the British forces while General Sullivan and General Nathanael Greene led the American forces. The British launched three major assaults on the Americans, but the day ended in a stalemate. Although the British thwarted the Americans, General Lafayette of the French fleet gave the Americans credit for their skilled escape from British entrapment, commenting that their getaway was the most successful action of the war.

It was at this battle where Rhode Island's black regiment made its first appearance under the command of Colonel Christopher Greene. The regiment, which was authorized by the General Assembly on February 6, 1778, helped lay the groundwork for the evacuation of the British from Rhode Island in October of 1779.

The Map of the Battle of Rhode Island is on loan from Rhode Island State Archives.

Nathanael Greene's Sword

Nathanael Greene, the youngest Brigadier General in the Continental Army, served through the Revolutionary War, becoming a close and trusted friend of General George Washington. He was one of only four Rhode Island leaders who rushed to offer their services to Washington when the first shot rang out in Lexington. Greene was made commander with the rank of Major General to Rhode Island's Army of Observation, and replaced General Horatio Gates as the leader of the Army in the South in 1780. He served his country until the end of the war, aiding the cause greatly by freeing South Carolina and Georgia from British rule.

Nathanael Greene's sword is on loan from the Rhode Island State House.

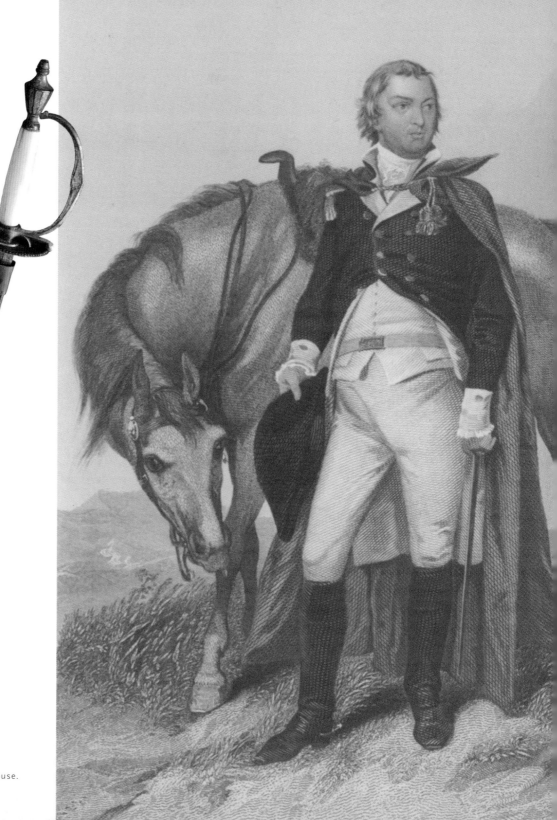

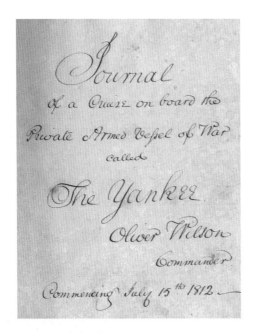

The War of 1812 and the Brig *Yankee* Journals

Captain Oliver Wilson sailed from Bristol harbor aboard an armed privateer in July of 1812, a month after the War of 1812 began. Wilson was in command of the brig *Yankee*, the most successful of America's privateers. The ship captured a total of $5,000,000 in property from 49 enemy vessels. The first cruise lasted three months, had a crew of 115, claimed ten prizes, and profited enough to provide each sailor with a $700 share. The success of this cruise set the standard for the following journeys. Many crewmembers came back with tales from each new venture, including Noah Jones, Captain Wilson's clerk. Jones sailed on the first two cruises, and kept a journal for each one. He wrote of pursuits and plunder of enemy ships as well as storms, whales, and his own feelings and thoughts. He concluded his adventures upon the brig *Yankee* noting; "Thus ends our cruise. Honor and shame from no condition arise. Act well your part, there all the Honor lies."

The brig *Yankee* journal is on loan from the Naval Historical Collection of the Naval War College in Newport.

The First Rhode Island Constitution

In answer to the "People's Constitution," (see page 17) the General Assembly of Rhode Island proposed a new constitution in March of 1842 called the "Landholders'" or "Freemen's Constitution." It granted suffrage and was in many ways similar to Dorr's constitution. It was defeated by a vote of 8,689 to 8,013, since many landholders voted against it.

A few months later another Constitutional Convention was called. The General Assembly proposed a Committee on Suffrage to study voter qualification issues. They adopted some features of the "People's Constitution" and struck the word "white" from Article II by a vote of 45 in favor to 15 opposed. Rhode Island was then the first state to grant black male citizens the right to vote. The delegates adopted the full Constitution on November 5, 1842. It came into law on the first Tuesday of May 1843, and remained the governing document of Rhode Island until 1986, when the next successful unlimited Constitutional Convention took place.

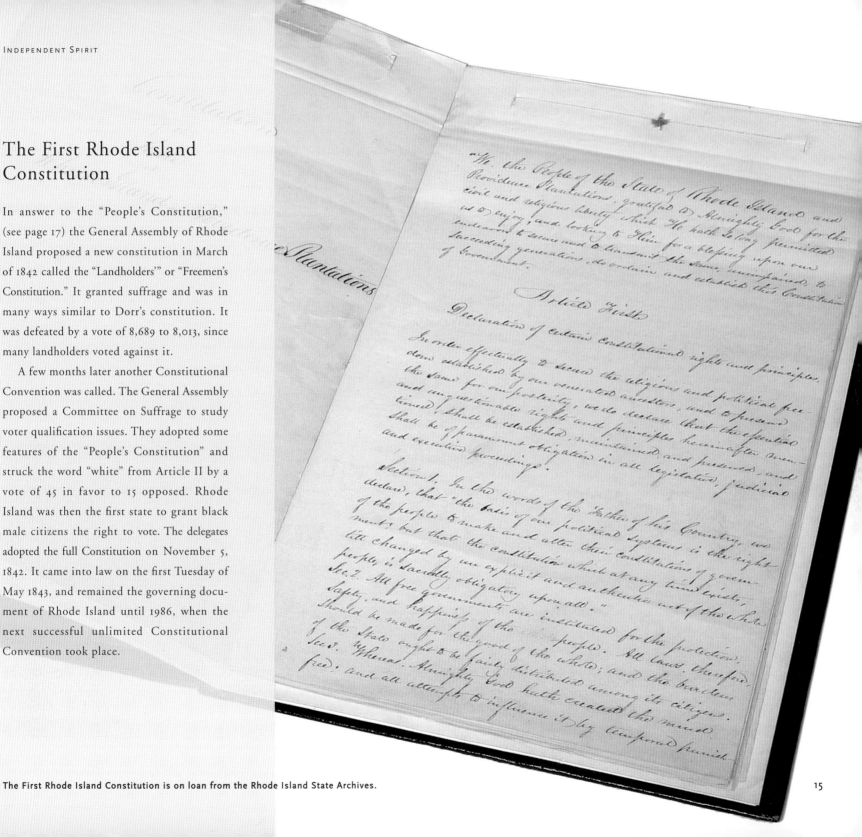

The First Rhode Island Constitution is on loan from the Rhode Island State Archives.

Thomas Wilson Dorr

Thomas Wilson Dorr, 1805-1845

Thomas Wilson Dorr was born in 1805 to a wealthy Providence manufacturer. Trained as a lawyer, he entered the state legislature in 1834. After 1840, as a leader of the Rhode Island Suffrage Association and its People's Party, he led a popular movement to extend voting rights to all adult males in the state regardless of whether they owned real estate. In 1841 the People's Party and the legislature sponsored two rival constitutional conventions. A majority of voters qualified under the old voting system voted for the People's Party constitution. Following rival elections in 1842, Dorr was one of two governors elected. Dorr tried to seize the Providence Armory — in the so-called Dorr's Rebellion. He fled the state but returned in 1843, and in 1844 was sentenced to life imprisonment at hard labor. He was released in 1845 because of ill health and died that year.

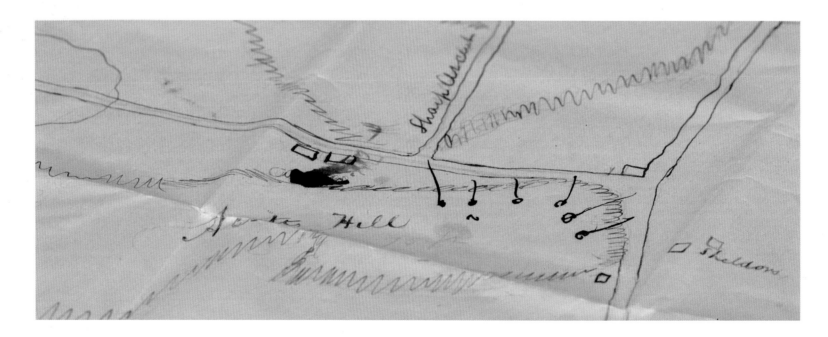

Painting of Thomas Wilson Dorr, courtesy of the Rhode Island Historical Society. The hand drawn map of Dorr's Rebellion is on loan from the Rhode Island State Archives.

Thomas Wilson Dorr and The People's Constitution

By the early 1800's every state except Rhode Island and Connecticut had adopted new constitutions giving their citizens full suffrage. These two states continued to adhere to their original charters, which limited voting rights to landowners and their eldest sons. Industrial expansion in Rhode Island created a new class of citizens who were not landholders, but made up a large portion of the population.

Thomas Wilson Dorr stood for what the general population desired in a government. He believed that at the conclusion of the Revolution the original 1663 charter should have been dissolved, and that the people of Rhode Island who had fought to obtain freedom from England should have the right to establish a constitution. On November 18, 1841, a "People's Constitution" was framed by Dorr's supporters in an unofficial "People's Convention." In December all persons declaring citizenship, of the age of twenty-one, and of state residence voted, and this unauthorized constitution was approved by a vote of 13,944 to 52.

Secretary's Copy

PROPOSED
CONSTITUTION
OF THE STATE OF RHODE-ISLAND AND PROVIDENCE PLANTATIONS,
AS FINALLY ADOPTED BY THE
PEOPLE'S CONVENTION,
Assembled in Providence, on the 18th day of November, 1841.

WE, the PEOPLE of the State of RHODE-ISLAND and PROVIDENCE PLANTATIONS, grateful to Almighty God for his blessing vouchsafed to the "lively experiment" of Religious and Political Freedom here "held forth" by our venerated ancestors, and earnestly imploring the favor of his gracious Providence toward this our attempt to secure, upon a permanent foundation, the advantages of well ordered and rational Liberty, and to enlarge and transmit to our successors the inheritance that we have received, do ordain and establish the following CONSTITUTION of Government for this State.

ARTICLE I.

Declaration of Principles and Rights.

1. In the spirit and in the words of ROGER WILLIAMS, the illustrious Founder of this State, and of his venerated associates, WE DECLARE, "that this government shall be a DEMOCRACY," or government of the PEOPLE, "by the major consent" of the same, "ONLY IN CIVIL THINGS." The will of the people shall be expressed by Representatives freely chosen, and returning at fixed periods to their constituents. This State shall be, and forever remain, as in the design of its Founder, sacred to "SOUL LIBERTY," to the rights of conscience, to freedom of thought, of expression and of action, as hereinafter set forth and secured.

2. All men are created free and equal, and are endowed by their Creator with certain natural, inherent and inalienable Rights; among which are life, liberty, the acquisition of property, and the pursuit of happiness. Government cannot create or bestow these rights, which are the gift of God; but it is instituted for the stronger and surer defence of the same; that men may safely enjoy the rights of life and liberty, securely possess and transmit property, and, so far as laws avail, may be successful in the pursuit of happiness.

3. All political power and sovereignty are originally vested in, and of right belong to the PEOPLE. All free governments are founded in their authority, and are established for the greatest good of the whole number. The PEOPLE have therefore an inalienable and indefeasible right, in their original, sovereign and unlimited capacity, to ordain and institute government, and, in the same capacity, to alter, reform, or totally change the same, whenever their safety or happiness requires.

4. No favor or disfavor ought to be shown in legislation toward any man, or party, or society, or religious denomination. The laws should be made not for the good of the few, but of the many; and the burdens of the State ought to be fairly distributed among its citizens.

5. The diffusion of useful knowledge, and the cultivation of a sound morality, in the fear of God, being of the first importance in a Republican State, and indispensable to the maintainance of its liberty, it shall be an imperative duty of the Legislature to promote the establishment of Free Schools, and to assist in the support of Public Education.

6. Every person in this State ought to find a certain remedy, by having recourse to the laws, for all injuries or wrongs which may be done to his rights of person, property or character. He ought to obtain right and justice freely and without purchase,

completely and without denial, promptly and without delay, conformably to the laws.

7. The right of the people to be secure in their persons, houses, papers and possessions, against unreasonable searches and seizures, shall not be violated; and no warrant shall issue but on complaint in writing, upon probable cause, supported by oath or affirmation, and describing, as nearly as may be, the place to be searched, and the person or things to be seized.

8. No person shall be held to answer to a capital or other infamous charge unless on indictment by a grand Jury, except in cases arising in the land or naval forces, or in the militia, when in actual service, in time of war or public danger. No person shall be tried, after an acquittal, for the same crime or offence.

9. Every man being presumed to be innocent, until pronounced guilty by the law, all acts of severity, that are not necessary to secure an accused person, ought to be repressed.

10. Excessive bail shall not be required, nor excessive fines imposed, nor cruel or unusual punishments inflicted; and all punishments ought to be proportioned to the offence.

11. All prisoners shall be bailable upon sufficient surety, unless for capital offences, when the proof is evident, or the presumption great. The privilege of the writ of Habeas Corpus shall not be suspended, unless when, in cases of rebellion, or invasion, the public safety shall require it.

12. In all criminal prosecutions, the accused shall have the privilege of a speedy and public trial, by an impartial jury; be informed of the nature and cause of the accusation; be confronted with the witnesses against him; have compulsory process to obtain them in his favor, and at the public expense, when necessary; have the assistance of counsel in his defence, and be at liberty to speak for himself. Nor shall he be deprived of his life, liberty or property unless by the judgment of his peers, or the law of the land.

13. The right of trial, by jury shall remain inviolate; and in all criminal cases the jury shall judge both of the law and of the facts.

14. Any person in this State, who may be claimed, to be held to labor or service, under the laws of any other State, territory, or district, shall be entitled to a jury trial, to ascertain the validity of such claim.

15. No man in a Court of common law shall be required to criminate himself.

16. Retrospective laws, civil and criminal, are unjust and oppressive, and shall not be made.

17. The People have a right to assemble in a peaceable manner, without molestation or restraint, to consult upon the public welfare; a right to give instructions to their Senators and Representatives; and a right to apply to those invested with the powers of Government for redress of grievances, for the repeal of injurious laws, for the correction of faults of administration and for all other purposes.

18. The liberty of the Press being essential to the security of freedom in a State, any citizen may publish his sentiments on any subject, being responsible for the abuse of that liberty;

Declaration of Independence

Ratified on July 4, 1776, this copy of the Declaration of Independence was delivered to Governor Nicholas Cooke of Rhode Island on July 6. The State of Rhode Island approved the Declaration on July 12, 1776 and the eloquently expressed freedoms were ordered to be published by Secretary of State Henry Ward. Following a thirteen cannon salute at Fort Liberty in Newport and another in Providence, the Declaration was presented to all Rhode Island towns to be read on the last Tuesday of August during their town meetings.

Solomon Southwick undertook the printing, releasing copies in two different forms. In the haste of printing, one version included an incorrect date: June 13, 1776 was printed instead of July 13, 1776. Secretary of State Henry Ward signed both.

Bill of Rights Ammendment to the Constitution, 1789

Betrayal of the British "Rights of Englishmen" during the Revolution fueled a fear of abuse on civil rights matters. Opponents of the Constitution demanded a "bill of rights" spelling out the protections of individual citizens, and on September 25, 1789 the First Congress of the United States proposed twelve amendments. The first two were not ratified. However, the last ten were approved by three-fourths of the state legislatures and these became the Bill of Rights.

Rhode Islanders feared the intrusion of a central government into their local autonomy, partly explaining why they refused to ratify the Constitution. The Bill of Rights was a major factor in Rhode Island's decision to finally ratify on May 29, 1790. This made the "first in war and last in peace" state the last of the original thirteen colonies to join the new union.

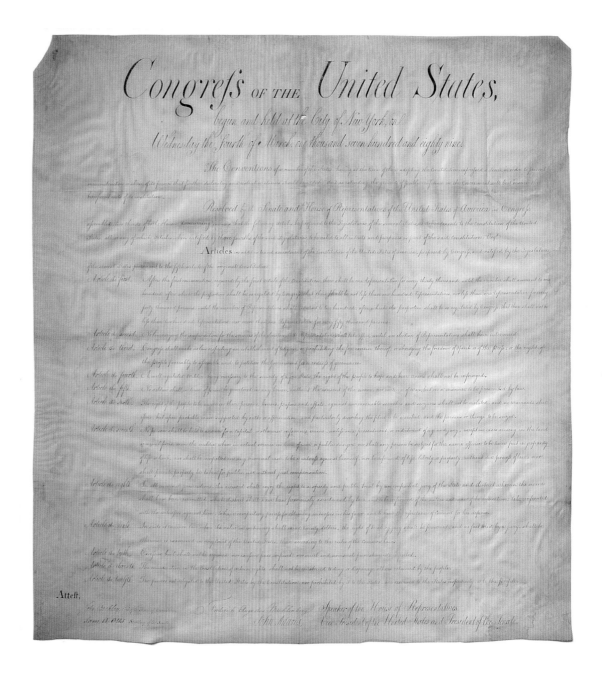

The Declaration of Independence and the Bill of Rights are on loan from the Rhode Island State Archives.

19

Photo of General Ambrose Burnside monument, courtesy of the Rhode Island Historical Society.

FIGHT FOR FREEDOM

World War I uniform hat is on loan from the Pawtuxet Valley Preservation and Historical Society.

Touro Synagogue

In 1658, Rhode Island's first Jewish settlers arrived in Newport from Barbados, seeking a refuge from religious persecution. As members of the diverse colonial Newport community, Jewish settlers were active participants in both cultural and commercial activities.

During their first 100 years in Rhode Island, members of the Jewish community took turns leading worship services in private homes. In 1758, the community hired Rev. Isaac Touro from Amsterdam, Holland, to lead the growing congregation. It was under the direction of Rev. Touro that the construction of a new synagogue began. Peter Harrison, a leading colonial architect, designed the building and charged no fee for the project he described as "a labor of love." Touro Synagogue was dedicated in 1763, and is recognized as the oldest synagogue in the United States.

In 1946, the United States Congress designated Touro Synagogue a National Historic Site, and in 2001 it became one of only 21 properties in the collection of the National Trust for Historic Preservation. Its artifacts and architecture remain essentially unchanged to this day.

Bill of Sale for Two Slaves

Even though the South is thought to have been the center of slavery, it was also prevalent in the North. Newport and Bristol, Rhode Island were the major slave markets of the American colonies. During the seventy-five years in which Rhode Island was active in the slave trade, whether legally or illegally, the numbers of slaves in the state steadily grew. In Rhode Island slaves labored in Narragansett as plantation families, in Middletown as crop workers, and in Newport as craftsmen. The Rhode Island Black Heritage Society is a resource for more information about slavery in Rhode Island.

Owners bartered, traded and sold their slaves as easily as they did livestock. This document illustrates the sale of two slaves from Thomas Arnold. They were traded for 21 barrels of cider and 10 shillings.

Moses Brown

John and Moses Brown

John and Moses Brown were members of a prominent Rhode Island family, founded by Chad Brown, who came to America from England in 1638 and was an elder of the First Baptist Church in America (founded by Roger Williams). For several generations the Browns were farmers, pastors, and surveyors, before James Brown, father of John and Moses, with his brother Obadiah, entered the West Indies trade, delivering livestock and food, acquiring rum and molasses, and transporting slaves from Africa. James Brown sent the first slave ship from Rhode Island in 1736. The second Brown family slave trading ship, sent out by Obadiah Brown and Company in 1759, was taken by privateers. After their third venture, the disastrous voyage of the ship *Sally*, in 1764, overrun with disease and a slave uprising, Moses Brown and two of his brothers gave up the slave trade.

Moses freed his slaves, became a Quaker, and was instrumental in founding the Providence Society for Promoting the Abolition of Slavery, which sued John for defiance of the new laws. John was acquitted. He sent the first ship from Narragansett Bay to China in 1787.

Plantation Owner, John Potter and Family, ca. 1740

This painting illustrates many of the attitudes and adornments that were important to the upper classes in the mid-18th century. Plantation owner John Potter chose to be portrayed with his finest clothing and wig, his refined and fashionable family, the newly popular ritual of tea drinking (with fine china and silver accessories), and a favorite house servant to illustrate his wealth and gentility.

"The Potter Family"

 Engraving of Moses Brown, courtesy of the John Hay Library at Brown University. "The Potter Family," a gift of Mrs. E. L. Winters, is on loan from the Newport Historical Society.

1784 Act Authorizing the Manumission of Negroes, Mulattoes, and Others, for the Gradual Abolition of Slavery

Slavery in Rhode Island can be dated as early as May, 1652 when the first recorded anti-slavery legislation was passed. This law did little good, however, as it was hardly observed or enforced.

Freedom came gradually for slaves in Rhode Island. In 1774 Rhode Island became the first state to prohibit the importation of slaves. During the Revolutionary War, men earned their freedom by enlisting in the famous Black Regiment. After the Revolution, The Act of Manumission of 1784 was passed by the Rhode Island General Assembly. The Act freed all slave children who were born after March 1, 1784 and who had served an apprenticeship until age 18 (for women) or age 21 (for men). The Act did not free all slaves immediately, but it would not be the last piece of anti-slavery legislation to be passed. Sadly, abolition legislation did not effectively end mistreatment of, or prejudice against, people of color.

The 1784 Manumission Act is on loan from the Rhode Island State Archives.

Abolitionist Elizabeth Buffum Chace, 1806-1899

Elizabeth Buffum Chace was an activist for such causes as the abolition of slavery, women's rights, prison reform, and the care of children. Her home in Valley Falls was a station on the "underground railroad" for runaway slaves. She was a founder of the Rhode Island Woman Suffrage Association, and its president for 29 years until her death at the age of 93. She kept this scrapbook documenting the Movement and her role in it. On March 12, 2002 she became the first Rhode Island woman to be honored with a marble sculpture to be permanently displayed at the State House.

The Elizabeth Buffum Chace scrapbook is on loan from the John Hay Library, Brown University.

Washington, July 3, 1862.

Gov. E. D. Morgan

My dear Sir—

I should not want the half of three hundred thousand, new troops, ~~men~~, if I could have them now. If I had fifty thousand additional troops here now, I believe I could substentially close the war in two weeks. But time is every= =thing; and if I get fifty thousand new men in a month, I shall have lost twenty thousand old ones during the same month, having gained only thirty thousand, with the difference between old and new troops still against me— The quicker you send, the fewer you will have to send. Time is ev= ery thing— Please act in view of this— The enemy having given up Corinth, it is not wonder= ful that he is thereby enabled to check us for a time at Richmond—

Yours truly

A Lincoln.

"To Union Governors" Letter from Abraham Lincoln, July 3, 1862

On July 2, 1862 Governor Edwin D. Morgan of New York telegraphed President Abraham Lincoln, "Is the call for 300,000 or for 200,000 volunteers? It appears in all the New York papers for 300,000." On the same day Lincoln replied, "It was thought safest to mark high enough. It is three hundred thousand." The next day Lincoln addressed a letter to Governor Morgan stating the urgent need for new troops now. Governor Morgan's name was crossed out by Edwin Stanton, Secretary of War, who also added "private and confidential" and inserted "Yours truly" before Lincoln's signature. The letter was then telegraphed to the governors of all Union states with the recognition that the problem raised by Morgan was one faced by all.

General Ambrose Burnside (seated at center)

General Ambrose Burnside, 1824-1881

Born in Indiana, Ambrose Everett Burnside settled in Bristol, Rhode Island as a manufacturer of firearms. During the Civil War he served first as a colonel in the Rhode Island Volunteers, then as brigadier general in the Union Army, as commander of the Army of the Potomac, and later in charge of the Army of Ohio. He resigned his position in 1865 after a failed mission at Petersburg, returning to Rhode Island where he would serve as governor three times and as United States Senator until his death in 1881. He is buried in Swan Point Cemetery on the east side of Providence.

One of Burnside's legacies is the term "sideburns" which came from the peculiar whiskers that he popularized during the Civil War era.

Civil War Drum

Marking the pace of the advancing Company A, 7th Rhode Island Volunteers, William Greene served as its drummer. He had been transferred to the company from Company C of the 7th who he had fought for in September of 1862. He was present at the Battle of Fredericksburg that took place on December 13, 1862. He died on April 21, 1863 while serving his country and fighting to preserve the Union.

World War I Uniform

By the time the United States entered World War I in 1917, France and England had already experienced trench warfare and several grim winters. Aware of this, West Point Academy sought uniforms for the winter months that would provide warmth and durability with as little weight as possible. An olive drab wool uniform was determined to be the most suitable. The 28,000+ Rhode Islanders who joined the army were provided with these uniforms as they left for war.

World War I uniform on loan from the Pawtuxet Valley Preservation and Historical Society. World War I diary is from a private collection.

JULY 1, 1894.

ARCHITECTURE

McKim, Mead and White

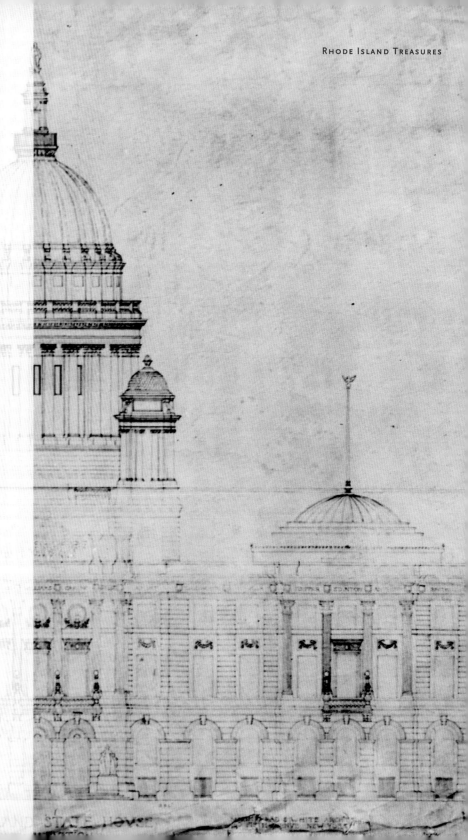

The Rhode Island State House

In his first governor's message in January, 1890, Governor Herbert W. Ladd noted the need for a new capitol building. Rhode Island needed a structure that reflected the state's aspirations and the pre-eminence of Providence as the second city of New England.

A State House Commission was created to oversee a competition of architecture firms. Competitions were a common means of selecting an architect for a major public building. The State House Commission's two-tiered selection process was unusual, however. The first call for entries, which began in November of 1890, was limited to Rhode Island architects as a way to ensure the fair representation of local talent. The second phase reviewed submissions from firms in New York and Boston.

During the fall of 1890 Governor Ladd corresponded confidentially with the New York firm of McKim, Mead and White. Fellow commission member Rowland Gibson Hazard had commissioned them to build the Narragansett Casino in the 1880's, and would hire them again in 1892 to build his own house in Narragansett. The commission engaged Richard Morris Hunt, the dean of American architects and a close friend of McKim, and Professor A.D.F. Hamlin of Columbia University, formerly of McKim, Mead and White as advisors. It seemed that the New York firm was destined to be chosen from the beginning.

Construction of the State House on Smith Hill began in 1895, and the building was occupied during the winter of 1900-1901.

Original plans for the Rhode Island State House on loan from the State Archives.

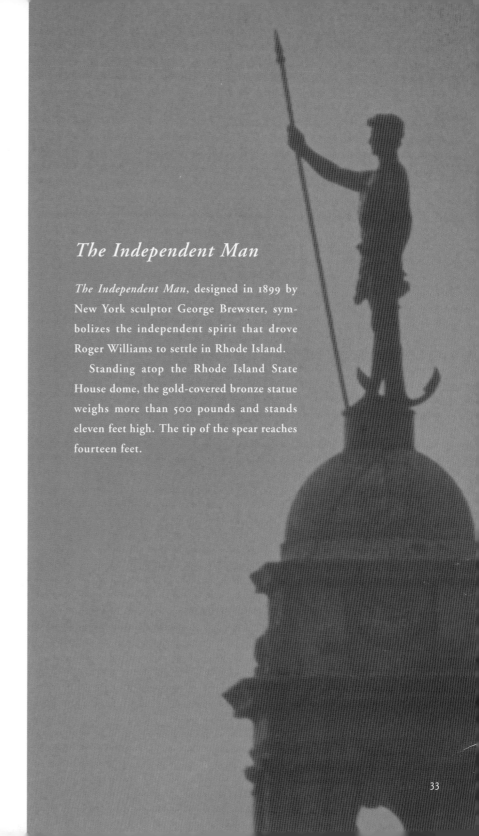

The Independent Man

The Independent Man, designed in 1899 by New York sculptor George Brewster, symbolizes the independent spirit that drove Roger Williams to settle in Rhode Island.

Standing atop the Rhode Island State House dome, the gold-covered bronze statue weighs more than 500 pounds and stands eleven feet high. The tip of the spear reaches fourteen feet.

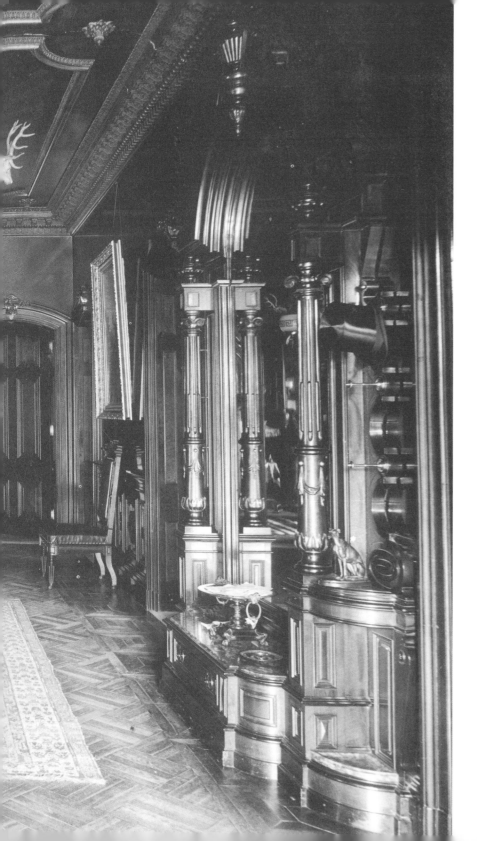

Governor Henry Lippitt House

The Governor Henry Lippitt House Museum on the east side of Providence has been lauded by the New York Times as one of the most complete, authentic and intact Victorian houses in the country.

Governor Henry Lippitt held Rhode Island's top post from 1875-1877. His home, completed in 1865, is a Renaissance Revival mansion. The interior craftsmanship includes richly carved woodwork, colorful stenciling, faux marble, and dazzling stained glass windows. The museum was designated as a National Historic Landmark in 1976 and donated by the Lippitt family to the Heritage Trust of Rhode Island (now Preserve Rhode Island) in 1981. The house is now open to the public for tours.

Photos courtesy of the Lippitt House Museum.

The Breakers

No architectural achievement sums up the Gilded Age better than the Vanderbilts' 1895 Renaissance-style palazzo, *The Breakers*.

The Breakers sits on an 11-acre estate on a cliff overlooking the Atlantic Ocean, where waves crashing on the rocks below gave the house its name. The estate is owned and managed by The Preservation Society of Newport County, and is open to the public for tours.

The "new" *Breakers* was built along the cliffs of Newport to replace the Vanderbilts' picturesque shingle cottage by Peabody and Stearns that had been destroyed by fire. Cornelius Vanderbilt chose architect Richard Morris Hunt, dean of American architects, for the rebuilding. After initial consideration of a French Renaissance chateau plan, Mr. Vanderbilt and Mr. Hunt decided on an Italian Renaissance palazzo theme, based on Genoese prototypes.

Construction began in the spring of 1893, and the 70-room house was formally opened the evening of August 14, 1895. The "new" *Breakers* features interiors by Allard and Sons of Paris, architect Richard van der Boijen and Ogden Codman.

Richard Morris Hunt, 1827-1895

Richard Morris Hunt is considered one of the fathers of American architecture. His works include the pedestal for the Statue of Liberty, the Metropolitan Museum of Art, and the Tribune Building in New York. He also designed many summer homes, including Newport's *The Breakers*, for such aristocrats as the Vanderbilts and the Astors. Sadly, Hunt died at his own Newport summer cottage one week before the formal opening of *The Breakers*. He is buried in the family plot at Newport's Island Cemetery.

This cast bronze portrait of Richard Morris Hunt is by Karl Bitter (American, 1867-1915). The medallion depicts Hunt's right profile and is inscribed "Rich.Morris.Hunt.A.D. 1891." It was commissioned by Mrs. William K. Vanderbilt as a tribute to the architect and was presented to Hunt and his family. The casting was done by the Henry Bonnard Bronze Co., New York in 1891.

VIEW OF THE RAILROAD DEPOT, PROVIDENCE, R. I.

Thomas Tefft, 1826-1859

Thomas Tefft was a Rhode Island schoolteacher when he met his mentor, the school reformer Henry Barnard, who recognized his talents and encouraged him to study architecture. His precocity was confirmed when he designed the Union Depot in Providence during his freshman year at Brown University. As a student, Tefft worked as a draftsman for the architectural firm of Tallman and Bucklin, and opened his own practice upon graduation. Five years later, he embarked for Europe where he studied firsthand the architecture that had influenced his work, but which he had only known through his vast collection of books. While in Florence, he fell ill and died at the age of thirty-three.

Tefft was an early member of the American Institute of Architects and an advocate for the establishment of American schools of art and architecture. His greatest ambition was to raise the level of American architectural design to rival that of Europe. His work includes a variety of building types: houses, public and commercial buildings, churches, libraries — many in the Italianate round-arched style that he pioneered in America.

PRIMARY SCHOOL IN WAKEFIELD, CA. 1844-48

This perspective is the only extant drawing of any of Tefft's one-room school houses. The building was probably meant to be brick, stuccoed brick, or clapboard. There is no date on the drawing, but it most likely belongs to the group of one-room school houses designed between the years 1844 and 1848. In this drawing Tefft uses, probably for the first time in a school design, the round-arched windows which came to characterize most of his later school designs.

COTTAGE FOR MISS EMILY HARPER, CA. 1853

Quite modest in scale and obviously intended for a shoreline site, this seaside house has a low, broad profile, with a wittily wave-like sloping mansard roof. Tefft employed shingles on the cottage exterior, a practice he described in his lecture "Rural Art" as one of the "truthful" ways to build with wood.

PROJECT FOR MERCHANTS' EXCHANGE, 1856

This design for a Merchants' Exchange in the commercial center of Providence was Tefft's last commercial project before his final departure for Europe in late 1856. It unfortunately was never built.

Original Tefft drawings and Union Station engraving, courtesy of the John Hay Library, Brown University.

T.A.Tefft Arch.

Primary School in Wakefield

MISS EMILY HARPER'S COTTAGE

Cottage for Miss Emily Harper

Merchants' Exchange

MERCHANTS EXCHANGE

Barrington Paver Bricks

Brick making, an industry that had been dormant since the first decade of the 19th century, reemerged and subsequently greatly influenced the town of Barrington's economic development. In 1847, the Nayatt Company, a group of Providence businessmen, purchased the clay pits in the south-central section of town and began construction of a large-scale factory that used steam-powered machinery. Scows and tugboats carried bricks along the Mouscochuck Creek Canal to the Providence River and then to urban markets.

Fundamental changes began to take shape in the 1850's with the arrival of the railroad and expansion of the brick making industry. In ensuing decades, Barrington was transformed from a sleepy agricultural town to a residential suburb and summer resort destination popular among residents of the industrial and commercial cities of Providence and Pawtucket. The New England Steam Brick Company facilitated further population growth, attracting French-Canadian and Italian immigrant workers. The new houses and roads, and the civic, religious, institutional, and commercial construction associated with this expansion all helped to change the face of the Rhode Island.

Barrington Paver bricks from The Barrington Preservation Society.

Photo of newspaper delivery boys, courtesy of Providence City Hall.

INDUSTRY AND TECHNOLOGY

Slater Mill in Pawtucket, 1789

Revolution in Pawtucket

In 1789 Samuel Slater, an English mechanic, left his native country for America. His partnerships with Moses Brown and William Almy gave him the opportunity to establish himself as a prominent player in the birth of the textile industry in the United States. In 1793, they constructed the first water powered cotton spinning mill in North America, in Pawtucket, Rhode Island. This was America's first factory. Considered the father of the United States textile industry, Samuel Slater eventually built several successful cotton mills in New England and established, with his brother John, the first planned industrial community in the country — Slatersville, Rhode Island.

Since America had not yet discovered great deposits of coal, factories were primarily water powered. Before the Civil War, textile manufacturing was the most important industry in America, with Rhode Island's technological advances keeping it on the cutting edge.

Carding Machine

Slater Mill in Pawtucket, Rhode Island was the first manufactory in North America to use the power of water for cotton production. In 1793, a dam was built to harness the power of the Blackstone River, which went on to become the hardest working river in America. Textile manufacturing became one of the United States' major industries, and the backbone of Rhode Island's economy.

The first automated carding machine in North America was of English origin. It was used to straighten cotton fibers so they could be spun into thread. This machine was the piece of equipment that Samuel Slater and his co-workers had the most difficulty replicating from English models.

Carding machine is on loan from Slater Mill.

Wilkinson Mill's Water Wheel

This working water wheel shows how power is generated using the force of a flowing river. The wheel is still used to produce power for the machine shop at the mill as part of the Slater Mill educational experience. Water flows from the river, through a specialized man-made channel called a raceway, and turns the water wheel. It then powers a central shaft rising through the mill. Gears attach this shaft to line shafts that are connected to the individual machines by belts made of leather or rope. This wheel at the Wilkinson Mill (part of the Slater Mill) powered three floors of textile machinery.

Maypole Braider

Built in 1872 by the New England Butt Company in Providence, the maypole braider demonstrates an aspect of specialization within the textiles industry. Threads from the spindles are interwoven, as in a maypole dance (hence the name), around a core thread or wire that is drawn through the center of the machine. While this early model was hand operated, by the turn of the 20th century braiders had become mechanized. They were used to produce thousands of miles of home and industrial wiring at a time when cities and towns were transitioning to electrical power.

The maypole braider is on loan from Slater Mill. Photos by Beau Jones.

Life in the Mills

In the 19th century, it was a widely accepted practice to employ children, often as young as four years old, to work in textile mills. Samuel Slater, creator of America's first textile mill, hired orphans and poor children who were wards of the town, paying them as little as 25 cents a week.

By 1830, 55% of mill workers in Rhode Island were children. The six-day work week started before sunrise and ended after sunset each day. Air in the mills was full of debris that caused respiratory disease. Mills were cold and drafty in winter and hot and humid in summer.

It wasn't until 1938, with the passage of the Fair Labor Standards Act, that child labor was effectively eliminated.

Nathanael Herreshoff, 1848-1938

At age 16, Nathanael Greene Herreshoff built his first steam engine. This engine and his approach to its design garnered considerable attention from the faculty and the president of the Massachusetts Institute of Technology, where he went to study two years later. After graduation Herreshoff was hired by George Corliss of Providence, the most prominent steam man of the era.

It was at Corliss where Nat was awarded his first of eight steam engine patents. He also designed marine engines and boats built by his blind older brother John Brown Herreshoff. Eventually, Nat joined his brother full time in the boat building business, the Herreshoff Manufacturing Company. Herreshoff was internationally recognized as one of the first developers of fast steam powered vessels and the marine engines that ran them. During its seventy years, the company built over 1,800 sail and power vessels ranging from eight-foot prams to a 160-foot steel schooner, and eight America's Cup winners. Rescued at auction in 1924 by the Haffenreffer family, the company went on to build 100 World War II fighting vessels. It closed in 1945.

HERRESHOFF STEAM LAUNCH ENGINE

Built in 1893, Nathanael Herreshoff's steam engine, including firebox, boiler, and single cylinder engine, was designed for his own personal use in a 22-foot launch. Damaged by the 1938 hurricane at the Herreshoff home in Bristol, it was restored to operating condition by Henry Luther of Warren.

The Herreshoff steam launch engine, courtesy of the Herreshoff Marine Museum in Bristol.

Gorham Silver

Gorham Silver was founded in 1831 by Jabez Gorham in Providence, Rhode Island. His son, John Gorham, followed in his father's footsteps, manufacturing coin, sterling and silver plate flatware and hollowware.

Gorham dominated American silver from the late 19th to the early 20th century. Their skilled artisans were often called upon to create such important objects as Mrs. Abraham Lincoln's tea set and presentation pieces for foreign dignitaries and heads of state. Today, guests of the White House are served with Gorham silver flatware. Sports awards such as the Davis Cup for tennis and the America's Cup for yachting were also designed and manufactured by Gorham.

Gorham Silver continues to operate in Smithfield, Rhode Island.

The Jewelry Industry

The jewelry manufacturing industry began in Providence in the late 1700's. Though there were no native sources of materials, there were wealthy ship captains, and traders who were interested in the silver and gold they collected on their voyages.

Seril Dodge, one of the most significant craftsmen in the area, settled in Providence in 1784, and started his business as a clock and watch maker. Ten years later he began to offer jewelry, such as gold necklaces, silver plated shoe and knee buckles, and pins and lockets. Dodge was the first to develop plated gold in Providence. He eventually sold his home and business to his half-brother, Nehemiah.

By 1805, three other firms had joined Nehemiah Dodge in Providence. They were John C. Jencks, Pitman and Dorrance, and Ezekiel Burr, all of whom turned to cheap jewelry manufacturing. The introduction of techniques such as rolled gold plate and gold filled expanded their capabilities. Though lower in quality than solid gold, they were also lower in price. Local development of suppliers to the jewelry industry gave Providence a further advantage, as most necessary materials were available right at home.

Today, Rhode Island remains the "jewelry capital of the world," with 25% of the U.S. jewelry industry concentrated here. Over 27,000 people are employed in jewelry manufacturing, distribution and related services. More than 1,000 companies are engaged in the manufacture and sale of such products as precious metal and fashion jewelry, crystal, military insignia, pens, key chains and awards.

Photos of bench workers courtesy of the Providence Jewelry Museum. Rings findings board and machinery photos by Beau Jones.

engraving machine

rotary shear, or slitting machine

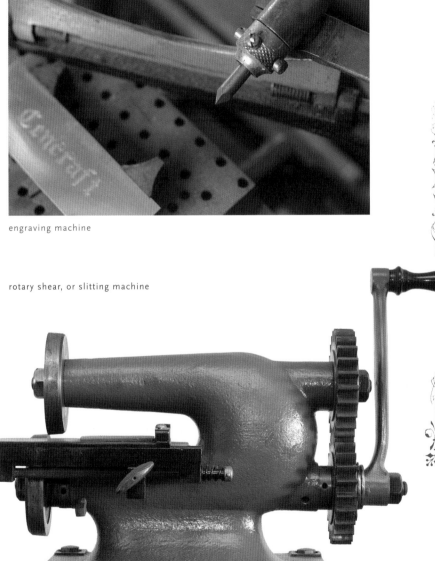

ESTABLISHED, 1849.

HENRY BLUNDELL & CO.,

MANUFACTURERS OF

Jewelers' Tools and Special Machinery.

OFFICE AND MANUFACTORY,

Nos. 35, 37 and 39 Clifford St., Providence, R. I.

No. 2 STANDARD ROTARY SHEAR.

On Iron Column. Combined Weight, 150 Lbs.

These Shears will cut from a fine tissue paper to No. 12 Brass Stock. The Gears are made from the best Bronze Metal. The Cutters are 4 x ¾, and of the best Tool Steel, and warranted in every respect.

Machine tools and advertisement on loan from the Providence Jewelry Museum.

Marc Harrison
and the Cuisinart

The original design from the late 1970's for
the Cuisinart food processor is attributed to
Marc Harrison, an industrial design professor at the Rhode Island School of Design. As
a result of a childhood accident, Harrison
was especially sensitive to the needs of people
with disabilities. He designed the Cuisinart
with large buttons that were easy to press,
lettering that could be easily read, and easy-
to-grip handles. The success of the Cuisinart
opened the door for Harrison to provide the
industry with countless other design solutions.

With his quick wit and passion for teaching, Harrison was a well-loved professor. He
dedicated 39 years of his life to the Rhode
Island School of Design before he died at the
age of 62 from Lou Gehrig's disease.

50

1954 advertisement courtesy of the Providence Jewelry Museum.

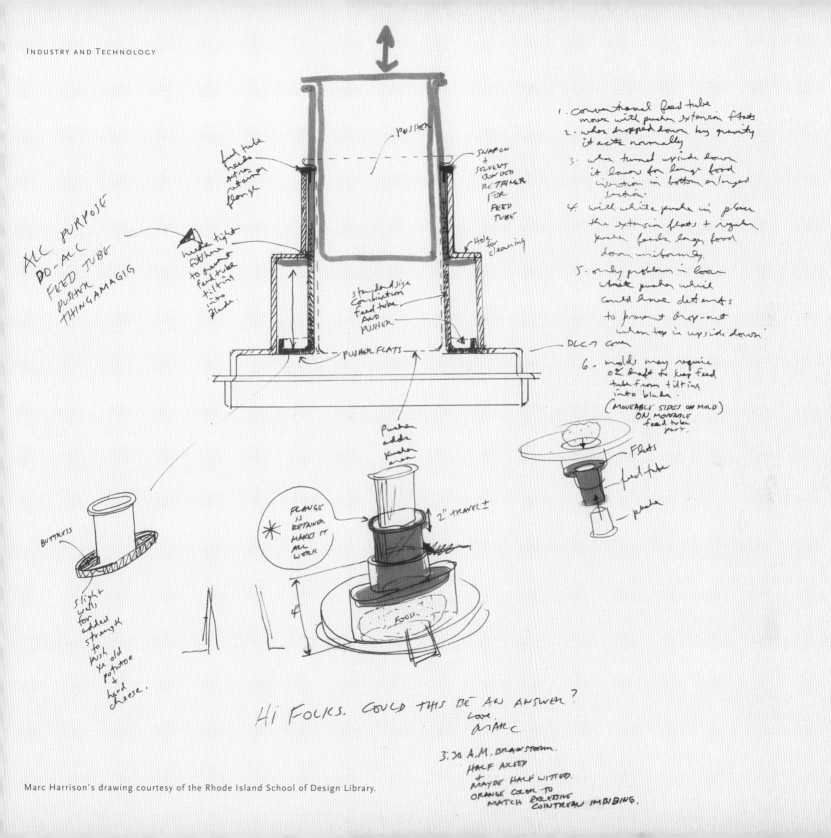

ALL PURPOSE
DO-ALL
FEED TUBE
PUSHER
THINGAMAGIG

1. conventional feed tube move with pusher extension flats
2. when dropped down by gravity it acts normally
3. when turned upside down it lowers for large food insertion in bottom enlarged section
4. with white pusher in place the extension flats & regular pusher feeds large food down uniformly.
5. only problem is lower white pusher which could have detents to prevent drop-out when top is upside down.
6. molds may require 0° draft to keep feed tube from tilting into blade. (MOVEABLE SIDES ON MOLD) ON MOVEABLE feed tube part.

HI FOLKS. COULD THIS BE AN ANSWER?
Love
MARC

3:30 A.M. BRAINSTORM.
HALF ASLEEP
& MAYBE HALF WITTED.
ORANGE COLOR TO MATCH EXISTING COINTREAU IMBIBING.

Ship's figurehead courtesy of a private collector. Photo by Beau Jones.

LEGACY AT SEA

Photo of shipwreck and fishermen, courtesy of the South County Museum.

Figurehead from the *Mary Gardiner*

Throughout time the figurehead of a ship was thought to embody the spirit of the vessel and to provide a safe voyage for those who sailed upon it. Though they have fallen out of use, figureheads once adorned the prow of every ship. This one is from the schooner *Mary Gardiner*, built in Wickford, Rhode Island. It was carved in the likeness of Mary Gardiner, wife of the ship's captain, Charles Gardiner. Its lender is the great great granddaughter of Mary Gardiner.

Bristol, Rhode Island

Figurehead is on loan by the South County Museum and Mrs. Anita Hinckley Hovey.

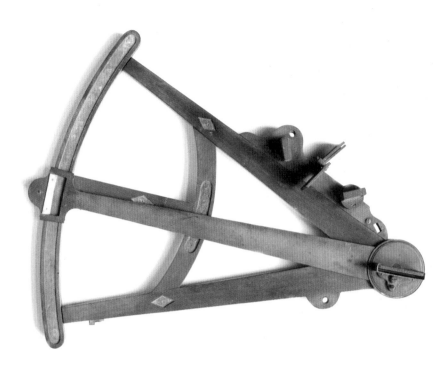

Hadley Quadrant

John Hadley first developed the quadrant in 1730 in London. Hadley was an English mathematician who invented the reflecting telescope. This quadrant, which measures the altitude of celestial bodies, was mainly used at sea to determine a ship's position. The instrument must be held upright with the index arm able to swing so that the glass can reflect the Sun. This design would evolve into the sextant, and is sometimes referred to as an octant. This quadrant was made in London for Captain Samuel Packard of Wickford, Rhode Island in 1785.

Fog Horn

Foghorns were used by fishermen to warn each other of ships passing too closely. This particular foghorn was used in the waters around Point Judith.

The Hadley Quadrant (above) and the foghorn (at right), are on loan from the South County Museum. The fog horn is a gift from Willard Kent.

John and Nathanael Herreshoff

John Brown Herreshoff started his shipbuilding business in 1863 in Bristol, Rhode Island. This remarkable blind boat builder created a partnership with his younger brother, Nathanael, in 1878. Together they produced incredible racing and cruising sailboats that measured up to 162 feet in length. They designed eight winning America's Cup boats, as well as the first United States Navy torpedo boats.

RELIANCE

The 144-foot *Reliance* was designed with bronze plating over steel frames, an aluminum deck, and a hollow steel mast. As the largest vessel ever to race for the America's Cup, she was an engineering triumph of her day. In the 1903 races she carried over 16,000 square feet of sail, the most sail ever to be carried by a single mast.

NYYC 30

The New York Yacht Club 30 Class (*NYYC 30*) was a 43-foot, six-inch gaff-rigged cutter. It was commissioned by members of the NYYC in 1904 for racing in Long Island Sound.

NYYC 30

Reliance   Photos courtesy of the Herreshoff Museum.

BUZZARDS BAY 12½′ SAIL BOAT

In the fall of 1914 the Herreshoff Company began construction on "The Wizard of Bristol's" design for a 12½′ boat. Nat had been asked to design and build a safe and seaworthy small boat for training youngsters on the waters of Buzzards Bay. The first group of 19 of the gaff-rigged "Buzzards Bay Boy's Boats" sailed in the season of 1915 and became an immediate success. In total, the Herreshoff Manufacturing Co. built 364 of these boats until ending production in 1943. Other builders have continued the design to this day, and the boat on display at the *Rhode Island Treasures* exhibition is still used in the summer sailing program at the Herreshoff Marine Museum.

FUN AND GAMES

Looff Carousel photos, courtesy of the East Providence Historical Society.

Amusement Parks

CRESCENT PARK

Boasting breath-taking rides, bathhouses, bandstand and a long dock to accommodate steamers, the new Crescent Park announced its arrival in the summer of 1886. George Boyden situated his park on Bullocks Point in Riverside, Rhode Island, where it became famously known as the "Coney Island of the East." It was the largest of Rhode Island's Victorian amusement parks, and as a vacation destination it included everything from boating and dancing to picnicking and the legendary Looff carousel. Advertising posters announced the thrills of the park and beckoned pleasure seekers to enter its gates.

The East Providence Historical Society has loaned images of Rhode Island's amusement parks.

LOOFF CAROUSEL

A masterful carver of carousels, Charles I.D. Looff was commissioned by Charles Boyden to create a carousel to showcase Crescent Park. The 62 hand-carved figures and four chariots he envisioned became the cornerstone of the park. New rides were added throughout the years, and as the park grew so did its popularity. Looff's son, also named Charles, built the shore dinner hall in 1914 and eventually became owner of Crescent Park in 1920. Looff expanded the park, adding a roller rink and the "Alhambra Ballroom."

LOOFF DRAGON

During the building stage of the Looff Carousel, Charles Jr. carved side panels for one of the sleighs. He formed them into dragons that were sadly never used on the actual carousel. These beautiful pieces are sculpted from raw basswood, and exemplify the intricate process behind the creation of the carousel rides.

The Carousel Park Commission has loaned two dragon side panels to Rhode Island Treasures.

East Providence, R. I. Crescent Park. The Merry-go-Round and Midway.

Crescent Park, Looff Carousel

HUNT'S MILLS

For the entertainment of their employees and their families, the Rumford Chemical Works, Glenlyon Print Works, and the Sayles Finishing Company opened an amusement park in 1900 called Hunt's Mills. Located in the Rumford section of East Providence, Hunt's Mills became popular very quickly, drawing park goers from all over Rhode Island. The cool wooded area along the Ten Mile River boasted a grand dance hall, carousel, midway, teahouse, picnic area, and canoeing.

Meeting the fate of so many of Rhode Island's beloved parks, it closed and its buildings were dismantled after a disastrous fire in 1925 destroyed the dance hall. Today the area is a beautiful park owned by the City of East Providence, and is the site of the John Hunt House Museum and the East Providence Historical Society.

ROCKY POINT

Rocky Point began as the location for Sunday outings for Captain William Winslow's passengers in the 1840's. He bought about 90 acres of land and opened a few amusements, a clam dinner hall, and flying horses. The second owner, Colonel Randall A. Harrington opened the site officially as Rocky Point. The Looff Ferris wheel, the Flume, and the Corkscrew were popular amusements until the park fell into bankruptcy in 1996. Most of the rides were auctioned off, and in the summer of 2000 the mayor of Warwick ordered the demolition of the rest of the park and declared the land "open space" for public use.

BOYDEN HEIGHTS

Boyden Heights came into existence eleven years after Crescent Park. George Boyden built his new park in 1900, about a mile and a half north of Narragansett Bay. Fashioned after European attractions, Boyden Heights featured beautiful romantic garden walkways, a shore dinner hall, and bandstand. A scenic railway provided views of the roller coaster, carousel, and polo field.

Hunt's Mills

VANITY FAIR

The grandest of all these parks was Vanity Fair. It opened in May of 1907 and featured its famed "Shoot the Chutes" ride that ended in a 1,600,000-gallon lagoon of water. It also included a grand ballroom, performing bears and a "Fighting the Flames" attraction with a building that burned several times a day and was extinguished by the "Vanity Fair Fire Company." It was the first park to charge admission — ten cents.

Unfortunately, its splendor lasted for the shortest time of any of the parks. A disastrous dancehall fire in 1912 led to the park's bankruptcy, just five short years after its opening. This early 20th-century version of Disney World sadly closed as a financial disaster.

Vanity Fair

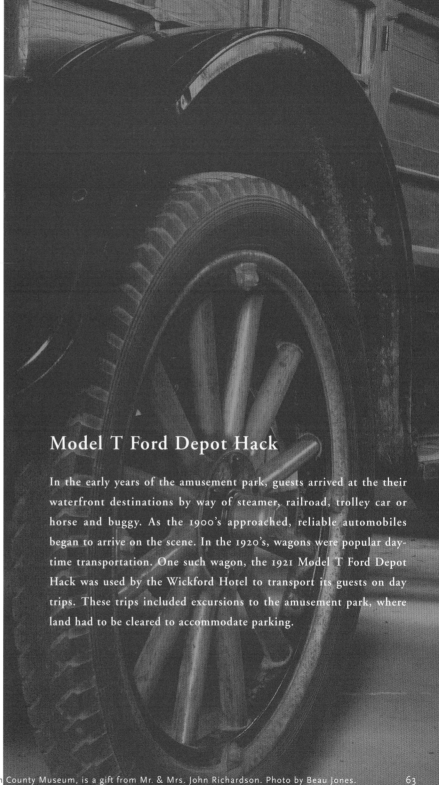

Model T Ford Depot Hack

In the early years of the amusement park, guests arrived at the their waterfront destinations by way of steamer, railroad, trolley car or horse and buggy. As the 1900's approached, reliable automobiles began to arrive on the scene. In the 1920's, wagons were popular day-time transportation. One such wagon, the 1921 Model T Ford Depot Hack was used by the Wickford Hotel to transport its guests on day trips. These trips included excursions to the amusement park, where land had to be cleared to accommodate parking.

The 1921 Ford Model T, courtesy of the South County Museum, is a gift from Mr. & Mrs. John Richardson. Photo by Beau Jones.

Ward. York. Gross. Start. G. Wright. Rourke. M.Greary. Kin

Farrell. Mathews.

Providence Grays photo from the Rhode Island Historical Society.

The Providence Grays and the First World Series

In 1871 the first baseball league, called the National Association, was formed. Other leagues, including the National League and the American Association, were created over the years. The first World Series was held in 1884 when the winner of the American Association, the New York Metropolitans, challenged the winner of the National League, the Providence Grays, to a three-game series.

The Grays accepted and swept all three games in the Metropolitans' home state. Grays' pitcher, Hoss Radbourne, led the team and went on to win 60 games that season. The Grays lasted until 1885 when they experienced their first losing season and spectator attendance dropped. However, in their eight years they had only one losing season and still stand as one of the greatest teams of the early years of baseball.

Brown University in the Rose Bowl

Perhaps the most memorable moment in Brown football history is the 1915 team's appearance in the Rose Bowl game. Brown did not have a particularly outstanding season in 1915, and ended with a 5-3-1 record. But a new star flashed across the field that year. Fritz Pollard ('19) was the first black to make coach Walter Camp's All-American Backfield. Unfortunately, Brown didn't win the game in Pasadena. On January 1, 1916, Brown was defeated by Washington State College, 14-0, in a heavy rainstorm, which hampered Pollard's performance.

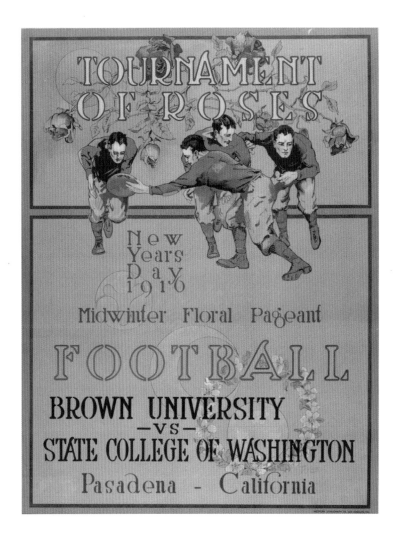

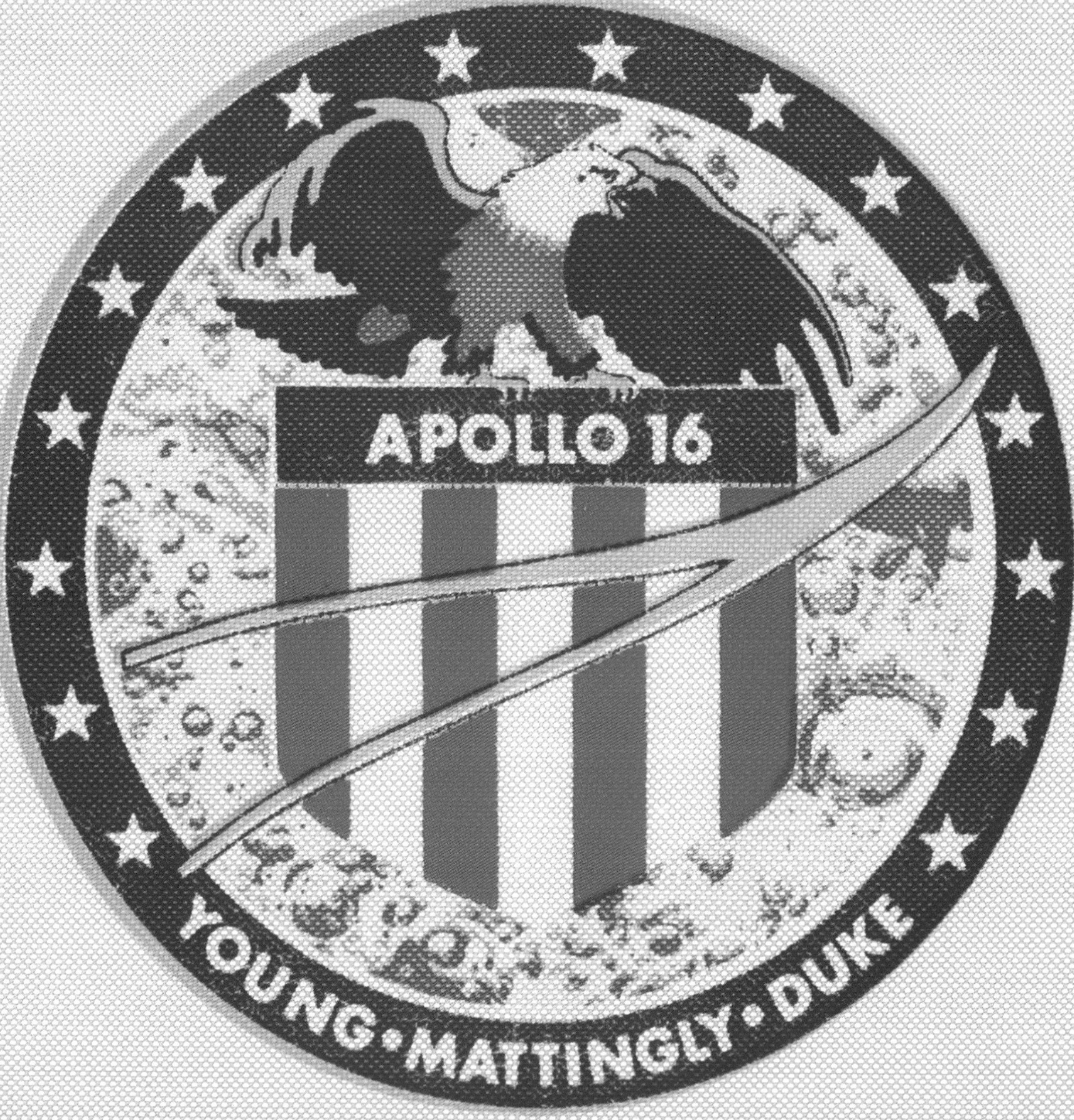
APOLLO 16
YOUNG • MATTINGLY • DUKE

DID YOU KNOW?

Rhode Island Red

The Rhode Island Red became the official state bird on May 3, 1954. Poultry farmers Isaac Wilbour and William Tripp are thought to have first developed this breed of chicken in Little Compton around 1854. A six-foot monument to the Rhode Island Red has stood in Little Compton since 1926. The breed is becoming increasingly rare due to cross-breeding. It is best known for being a robust producer of locally preferred brown eggs

This specimen of a Rhode Island Red traveled to the State House in 1994 and was honored in a ceremony commemorating the breed's 40th anniversary as our state bird.

This Rhode Island Red specimen is on loan from the Museum of Natural History at Roger Williams Park, Providence.

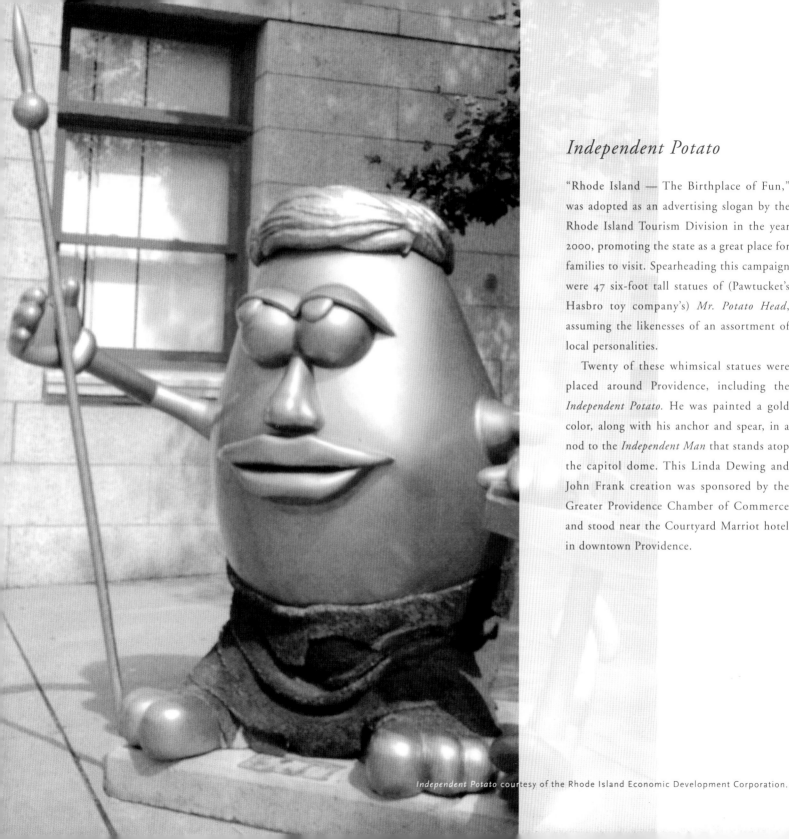

Independent Potato

"Rhode Island — The Birthplace of Fun," was adopted as an advertising slogan by the Rhode Island Tourism Division in the year 2000, promoting the state as a great place for families to visit. Spearheading this campaign were 47 six-foot tall statues of (Pawtucket's Hasbro toy company's) *Mr. Potato Head*, assuming the likenesses of an assortment of local personalities.

Twenty of these whimsical statues were placed around Providence, including the *Independent Potato*. He was painted a gold color, along with his anchor and spear, in a nod to the *Independent Man* that stands atop the capitol dome. This Linda Dewing and John Frank creation was sponsored by the Greater Providence Chamber of Commerce and stood near the Courtyard Marriot hotel in downtown Providence.

Independent Potato courtesy of the Rhode Island Economic Development Corporation.

Apollo Patches

Among the little known facts of Rhode Island history is that the Screen Print Corporation of Coventry produced the official insignia patches worn by Apollo astronauts.

As a result of the fatal 1967 launch pad fire, all materials used in the astronauts' suits, even their patches, had to be made of fire-resistant materials. Eastern Color and Chemical Company of Providence developed the flame-resistant ink. Nine colors were used in the printing, which was done under contract with the Owens-Corning Fiberglass Company of Cumberland.

A plaque displaying all of the patches was presented to President Richard Nixon from the residents of Rhode Island as a token of their pride in participating in the moon exploration program.

The Apollo patches are on loan from a private collector.

Shepard Fairey and the Andre the Giant Phenomenon

Shepard Fairey, a former student at the Rhode Island School of Design, first designed the infamous *Obey* stickers in 1989. This experiment proved the effect of advertising, as this "absurd icon" with the slogan *Obey* has been spotted across the country and even around the globe.

Since then Fairey's propaganda has turned into stickers, skateboards, clothing, posters, and a documentary film. He now works for Black Market, a Los Angeles firm, designing for such corporations as Pepsi and Universal Pictures. He still works on the *Obey* artwork that has become his signature.

Shepard Fairey's artwork, courtesy of the artist's family.

girls' cottage, ca. 1900

Orphanage photos courtesy of Rhode Island College.

Rhode Island College and The State Home and School Project, Rhode Island's First Public Orphanage

Rhode Island College, the state's oldest public institution of higher education, is celebrating is Sesquicentennial. Since its founding in 1854, the College, first known as the Normal School, then as Rhode Island College of Education, was founded for the purpose of professional education of teachers. Over forty years ago, the mission of the College grew to encompass programs in the arts and sciences, management and technology, nursing, and social work. Today the College offers over ninety degree programs. The State Home and School Project is but one way the College continues to fulfill its commitment to the past, present, and future.

On the grounds of what is now Rhode Island College's East Campus, one of America's first post-Civil War orphanages, The State Home and School, was founded in 1884. For nearly 100 years, until the late 1970's, children who were in the care of the state of Rhode Island lived at this location. It was called The State Home and School for Children, and later became known as The O'Rourke Children's Center. Rhode Island College acquired the buildings in the early 1990's.

While research was being conducted for Trinity Repertory Theatre's production of *The Cider House Rules*, records, ledgers, and artifacts were discovered in files at the Rhode Island Department of Children, Youth and Families. The history of the Home captured the attention of DCYF, the secretary of state, and the faculty and administration of Rhode Island College. It was decided that preserving the legacy of one of the oldest orphanages in the country was of national importance.

school room of the smallest children

The Forman Center, now the College admissions office;
formerly the superintendent's residence for the State Home and School

Music

Matilda Sissieretta Joyner Jones, 1869-1933

"The flowers absorb the sunshine because it is their nature. I give out melody because God filled my soul with it."

Matilda Sissieretta Joyner Jones, born in Virginia in 1869, was one of the best-known and highest-paid black singers in America. She moved to Providence with her family in 1876, where she attended Meeting Street and Thayer Schools and sang for the public at school functions and at Pond Street Church. Sissieretta married David Richmond Jones in 1883, and he became her manager. They divorced in 1899 after he reportedly squandered and mismanaged her money.

Sissieretta attended the New England Conservatory in Boston and began performing in front of much larger crowds in Boston and New York. She toured the West Indies with a black troupe and began to be known as "The Black Patti," compared to the Italian opera singer, Adelina Patti. She sang for President Benjamin Harrison in the White House and starred in the *Grand African Jubilee*, a three-day event at Madison Square Garden in New York.

After signing a contract with manager Maj J.B. Pond, Sissieretta charged $2000 per appearance, the highest fee ever paid to a black artist. She embarked on an extended tour of Europe and sang for the Prince of Wales and the Kaiser. She later formed "Black Patti's Troubadors," her own company, which toured for the next 20 years.

Sissieretta retired in 1916 in Providence, and died in 1933. By that time, her savings were nearly gone.

Sissieretta Jones' dresses are on loan from the Rhode Island Black Heritage Society.

George M. Cohan, 1878-1942

George M. Cohan was born in Providence on July 3, 1878 — not on the fourth of July, as the song says! His parents were travelling vaudevillians; with George and his sister Josephine, they were known as "The Four Cohans." As a very young man, Cohan began to write skits and songs for his family to perform, and soon began to write for other vaudeville acts as well.

Cohan's first full-length musical comedy was *The Governor's Son*, in 1900, which proved a successful touring vehicle for the Cohans for several seasons. George M. Cohan became a star player in his own right in his 1904 musical play *Little Johnny Jones*. In it, Cohan played what would become his signature character: the brash young American — the "Yankee Doodle Boy." The show featured the still-popular song "Give My Regards to Broadway."

Over the next few years, Cohan wrote and starred in the musicals for which he is best known, including *George Washington Jr.* (with the song "You're a Grand Old Flag") and *Forty-Five Minutes from Broadway* (including the title song and "Mary's a Grand Old Name").

Cohan also wrote non-musical plays, including the mystery *Seven Keys to Baldpate*, and patriotic songs during World War I, of which the best known is "Over There." In his later years he was praised for his portrayal of a small-town newspaper publisher in Eugene O'Neill's *Ah Wilderness!* and for his role as Franklin Delano Roosevelt in *I'd Rather Be Right*.

He was famously portrayed by James Cagney in the 1942 film *Yankee Doodle Dandy*. And in 1968, he was portrayed on the Broadway stage by Joel Grey in *George M!* which featured some of the best-loved of George M. Cohan's music.

George M. Cohan sheet music courtesy of the John Hay Library, Brown University.

Newport Jazz Festival

The Newport Jazz festival, originally sponsored by Mr. and Mrs. Louis Lorillard and produced by George Wein, has brought together jazz lovers and great figures of the jazz world since the first performance in July 1954. The festival has featured such performers as Louis Armstrong, Dave Brubeck, and Billie Holiday. In 1960, 1969, and 1971 the festival was marred by riots which caused performance cancellations.

Newport Jazz Festival programs and artifacts on loan from the Newport Historical Society.

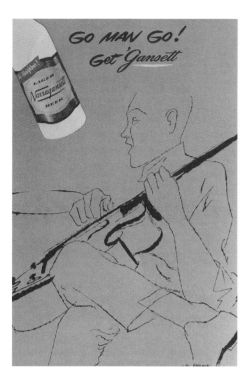

Newport Folk Festival

The Newport Folk Festival has been considered an American institution since it began. Founded by George Wein in 1959, it has served as a springboard for such talent as James Taylor, Joni Mitchell, Joan Baez, Janis Joplin, and Peter, Paul, & Mary.

The event was cancelled in 1971 due to growing social unrest, and 15 years later, was reinstated with many of the acts that made their start in Newport. Over the years, an effort was made to include up-and-coming artists, such as Mary Chapin Carpenter, the Violent Femmes, Bela Fleck, and the String Cheese Incident, as well as musicians who seemed to be a constant through the generations, like B.B. King, Sweet Honey in the Rock, and The Band.

Photo of Arlo Guthrie performing at the Newport Folk Festival, courtesy of the Newport Historical Society.

a 1969 photo of Liberace in Warwick (standing, center)

Tom Jones (center) with Larry and Jean Bonoff

The Warwick Musical Theater

Burton "Buster" Bonoff opened the Warwick Musical Theater in 1955 as an in-the-round tent. A permanent, though open-sided, structure was built in 1967, but locals continued to affectionately call it "The Tent." Bonnoff's son, Larry, later joined his father in the business. It was a popular destination for big-name summer entertainment for 45 years, until it closed at the end of the 1999 season.

LIBERACE

Of all the acts ever to grace the stage at the Warwick Musical Theater, Liberace was Larry Bonoff's favorite. He was one performer who gave the audience much more than their money's worth, including at least ten costume changes throughout the show. But, according to Bonoff, the best part of Liberace's visits was the man himself. Known to close friends as "Lee," it was "his love of life, friendships, and generosity as a human being that made knowing this man the most memorable of [his] experiences in show business," Bonoff said.

"When [his] parents visited Lee in Palm Springs, my mother took special time looking at one statue during their tour of the house. When they woke up the next morning, the statue was waiting for them at their hotel. Lee really enjoyed giving back more than anything in the world."

TOM JONES

Tom Jones played a major role in Larry Bonoff's entertainment career and life. "The biggest line at the theater was when Tom Jones tickets went on sale," he remembers. In 1972, Larry went on the road with Tom Jones as the entertainer's road manager. His time with Jones was Bonoff's "first opportunity to see the music business from the other side of the fence and to see what a great man Tom Jones was."

Bill Cosby with Larry Bonoff

Larry Bonoff (second from right) with The Beach Boys

Mick Jagger's Arrest

Boston-bound on a foggy summer night in 1972, Mick Jagger and Keith Richards of the Rolling Stones were stuck at T.F. Green airport in Warwick when they should have been warming up backstage. When they were approached by a photographer from the Providence Journal-Bulletin, the rock stars assaulted him and the police officer on duty, resulting in their arrest. The arrests initiated further altercations, ending with five men in custody charged with assault and obstruction of a police officer.

1922

Newport

Photo of Nancy Prophet, courtesy of Rhode Island College.

LITERATURE AND ART

Edgar Allan Poe, 1809-1849

Edgar Allan Poe, poet, editor, essayist, and short story writer, was born in 1809 to David and Elizabeth Arnold Poe, members of a repertory theatre company. Orphaned at an early age, he became the foster son of John and Frances Allan of Richmond, Virginia. As a young man, he became estranged from Allan owing to differences in outlook. His careers both at the University of Virginia and in the military were cut short because of financial problems.

Poe's first published work was *Tamerlane and Other Poems*, published anonymously in Boston in 1827. He continued to write poetry and short fiction for the next several years, and in 1835 his always precarious financial situation was remedied to a certain extent when he accepted a position with the monthly Richmond publication, the *Southern Literary Messenger*. Over the next decade, he continued to publish the poetry and short stories for which he is best known, including *The Raven* (1845), *The Fall of the House of Usher* (1839), and *The Black Cat* (1843).

In 1848, Poe visited Providence, where he became acquainted with the poet Sarah Helen Whitman, with whom he had been in literary correspondence. In November, Poe and Sarah Helen entered into a "conditional engagement": Poe was to cease drinking, and Sarah Helen would seek the approval of her mother (upon whom she was financially dependent) for their marriage. On November 13, Poe had this daguerreotype taken for Sarah Helen at the studio of Masury & Hartshorn, on what is now Westminster Street, near the corner of Memorial Boulevard.

Poe could not keep his promise to Sarah Helen; and the engagement was broken. In 1849, Poe died in Baltimore. He remains perhaps the best-known American poet of his time, whose works are translated into countless languages. Poe's detective stories inspired a new genre, in which his influence is still felt.

Edgar Allan Poe

Sarah Helen Whitman

The digital image of the Whitman daguerreotype of Edgar Allan Poe and the portrait of Sarah Helen Whitman and are on loan from the John Hay Library, Brown University.

Sarah Helen Power Whitman, 1803-1878

Sarah Helen Whitman was born in Providence on January 19 (the same day as Edgar Allan Poe), in 1803. She married John Power, a Boston lawyer, in 1828. Sarah Helen returned to live in Providence after her husband's death in 1833; her home on Benefit St. is still standing.

Sarah Helen wrote poetry and essays, and was an advocate of many reform movements of her day, notably women's rights and universal suffrage. She was interested in transcendentalism and spiritualism. Her home became a gathering place and a center for literary conversation.

In 1848, during her courtship with Edgar Allan Poe, the two visited the Athenaeum library. Sarah Helen asked Poe if he had read *Ulalume*, an unsigned poem that had appeared in a recent issue of a literary periodical. "To my infinite surprise, he told me that he himself was the author. Turning to a bound volume of the *Review* which was in the alcove where we were sitting, he wrote his name at the bottom."

This portrait in oils of Sarah Helen Whitman is by John B. Arnold.

Edgar Allan Poe and Sarah Helen Whitman

To Helen was written from Poe's memory of his first sight of Sarah Helen Whitman, one evening in July 1845, near her home on Benefit St. She wore a white dress and a gauzy white scarf on her head. Poe recognized Sarah Helen from a friend's description of her, but later refused an introduction because he thought the widowed Mrs. Whitman was still married.

In June, 1848, Poe sent an unsigned copy of the poem to Sarah Helen; she recognized his handwriting from previous correspondence. The poem was first published in the *Union Magazine* for November, 1848.

To Helen
by Edgar Allan Poe

Helen, thy beauty is to me
Like those Nicean barks of yore,
That gently, o'er a perfum'd sea,
The weary way-worn wanderer bore
To his own native shore.

On desperate seas long wont to roam,
Thy hyacinth hair, thy classic face,
Thy Naiad airs have brought me home
To the beauty of fair Greece,
And the grandeur of old Rome.

Lo! in that little window-niche
How statue-like I see thee stand!
The folded scroll within thy hand —
A Psyche from the regions which
Are Holy land!

H. P. Lovecraft, 1890-1937

Howard Philips Lovecraft was born on August 20, 1890, in the home of his maternal grandfather, Whipple Phillips, at 454 Angell Street on the east side of Providence. Except for his first three years, and two years of "exile" in New York (1924-1926), Lovecraft was to spend all of his life in his Providence. His identification with his beloved natal city was so strong that on his tombstone in Swan Point Cemetery is carved "I Am Providence."

Although he is now regarded, along with Edgar Allan Poe, as one of the founding fathers of American horror and science fantasy literature, Lovecraft spent most of his life writing in obscurity. His poems and short stories appeared mostly in amateur journals and pulp magazines, and only one novel was published before he died in 1937.

19th-Century Hair Sculpture

During the 1860's and 70's, artwork created with human hair was a popular tribute to a loved one who had passed away, or to celebrate a rite of passage, such as an engagement. Hair, from a living or a deceased person, or from an entire family, was often made into jewelry or woven into a wreath which was hung in a shadow box.

Working with hair was a very time consuming and tedious process. Hair was wrapped onto bobbins and then braided or macraméd. As the 19th century came to a close, hair wreaths became more elaborate, with china flowers or beads woven into them.

The donor's mother, Mrs. Nicholas Clark Reynolds of Exeter, made this piece.

The hair sculpture, a gift from Mrs. Harriette E. Lewis, is on loan from the South County Museum.

Gilbert Stuart, 1755-1828

Gilbert Stuart was born in Saunderstown, Rhode Island in 1755. After moving to Newport, where he showed early promise in painting, he received instruction from Cosmo Alexander, a Scottish painter whom he accompanied to Scotland in 1772. In 1775 he studied with Benjamin West in London, England, where he opened a studio and became one of the most sought-after portrait painters. He settled in Philadelphia in 1792, where he painted one hundred and twenty four portraits of George Washington. Stuart is best known as the creator of the image of George Washington that is on the American one-dollar bill.

Stuart painted this intense self-portrait in 1778 while studying with West in London. The portrait was given to his friend, Dr. Benjamin Waterhouse (an advocate of vaccination against smallpox). Mrs. Waterhouse donated the portrait to the Redwood Library.

Self-Portrait at Twenty-Four, 1778 by Gilbert Stuart is on loan from the Redwood Library and Athenaeum.

Edward Greene Malbone, 1777-1807

Edward Greene Malbone, born in Newport, Rhode Island in 1777, was a renowned as a portrait painter and miniaturist, and also painted landscapes. He painted in Providence, Boston, and Charleston, South Carolina and later in Europe, finally returning to America, where he enjoyed great success.

The Hours, painted on ivory, is Malbone's most famous miniature watercolor portrait. The three women represent the past, present, and future. After Malbone's early death, *The Hours* belonged to his sister, Mrs. Harriet Whitehorne. Upon her death, the painting was offered to the Providence Athenaeum for $1200. Elizabeth Bridgham Patten, daughter of the library's vice president, successfully raised the funds for its purchase.

In 1881 Frederick A. Potter and James Dunmanway (who was rumored to have been part of Jesse James's gang), stole *The Hours* from the Athenaeum. The library offered a $200 reward for the return of the painting. The thieves were apprehended and *The Hours* was returned to the Providence Athenaeum, where it remains to this day.

The Hours by Edward Greene Malbone (shown here at actual size) is on loan from the Providence Athenaeum.

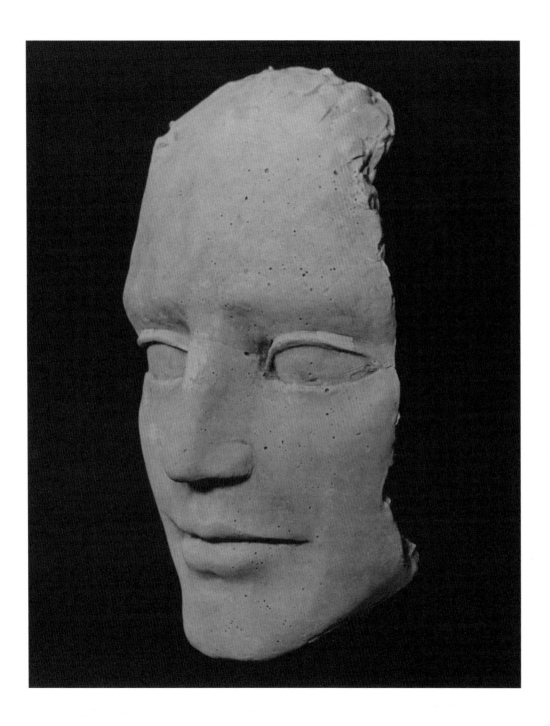

Nancy Elizabeth Prophet, 1890-1960

Nancy Elizabeth Prophet was born in 1890 in Providence, Rhode Island. Encouraged by family and friends, Prophet enrolled in the Rhode Island School of Design, working as a domestic to pay her tuition.

After graduation, she lived briefly in New York. In 1922, with the financial assistance of Gertrude Vanderbilt Whitney, she went to Paris to study. While in Paris, Prophet won the Harmon Foundation Prize, and exhibited her work at the Paris August Salons from 1924 until 1927 and at the Salon d'Automne in 1931 and 1932.

She returned to the United States, teaching at Spelman College in 1932, and at Atlanta University in 1937. As a black woman, she did not fit into the Atlanta art community, and, in 1945, returned to Rhode Island where she was unknown as an artist. Despite a one-person exhibition of her work in 1945 at the Providence Public Library, she died in 1960 in poverty and obscurity.

Nancy Elizabeth Prophet's work was featured in the 1978 exhibition at Bannister Gallery, Rhode Island College, titled, "Four From Providence."

Silence by Nancy Elizabeth Prophet is on loan from Rhode Island College.

Buttonwood Cove

Untitled

Edward Mitchell Bannister, 1828-1901

Edward Mitchell Bannister was born in 1828 in St. Andrews, New Brunswick, Canada. In 1848, after the death of his parents, he moved to Boston where he worked as a barber and began to paint. He married a woman of mixed Narragansett Indian and African American blood who was born in North Kingstown, Rhode Island. Both Bannisters were active in abolitionist circles in Boston before they moved to Providence in 1870.

Though Bannister's formal art education was limited, one of his paintings was accepted by the Philadelphia Centennial Exposition of 1876. *Under The Oaks*, as the painting had been named, was selected for the first prize medal. Upon the discovery of Bannister's African-American heritage, the judges wanted to "reconsider" the award, but the artist's competitors insisted that the decision be upheld. Bannister was awarded the medal.

Bannister was among Providence's leading 19th century painters. He was on the board of directors of the Rhode Island School of Design, and, in 1872, a founding member of the Providence Art Club.

Edward Mitchell Bannister's paintings are on loan from the Providence Athenaeum.

Treasures of Hope, by Maxwell Mays is on loan from the Providence Tourism Council.

Maxwell Mays

Maxwell Mays is perhaps one of Rhode Island's best known living artists. Born in Rhode Island and a product of the Rhode Island School of Design, he began his painting career when he was stationed in Recife, Brazil during World War II. With simple materials — crayons, a fountain pen, marking pencils and a child's paint set — he filled sketchbooks with the wonderful, crumbling examples of Dutch and Portuguese colonial architecture. He recognized that, very much like at home in Rhode Island, an important architectural heritage was being destroyed block by block in the name of progress. He recorded street scenes, push carts, parks, patios, fountains, front gates and carved doors. Mays was discovered by an art collector from Colorado who was a U.S. Navy officer. Their friendship resulted in Mays' first show at the museum in Colorado Springs, and then at the Denver Museum.

Returning to peacetime New England, he saw the once familiar scene in a new light, and painted enthusiastically. Eighteen pictures made up his first show at Ferargil Gallery on 57th Street in New York City. The show sold out. A summer in France the following year resulted in a second exhibition.

Maxwell Mays now lives and paints in a 1737 Rhode Island farmhouse that is filled with his work and with artifacts that often appear in his pictures. His series of cover pictures for *Yankee*, the New England magazine, has added to his recognition.

Carved Mahogany Card Table Attributed to John Townsend, 1733-1809

Rhode Island's colonial elite, including the Brown family of Providence and the Redwood family of Newport, amassed substantial fortunes through the maritime trades. Their homes were furnished with the work of Newport's leading cabinetmakers such as the Townsends and the Goddards. This table, attributed to John Townsend, is an excellent example of the masterful carving skills of Newport's craftsmen. Townsend stands as one of early America's premier cabinetmakers, with over thirty surviving examples of his labeled works.

The Townsend card table, a gift from Ellen F. Townsend, is on loan from the Redwood Library and Athenaeum.

A and L Tirocchi

From 1915 until 1947, Italian-born sisters Anna and Laura Tirocchi owned and operated A and L Tirocchi Dressmakers in Providence, Rhode Island. From their Victorian mansion at 514 Broadway, they served the elite women of Providence as custom dressmakers.

The dresses, coats, evening wraps and bathing suits that the Tirocchi sisters created reflected the times. America had entered a prosperous era following World War I. The stock market was booming. Women were given the right to vote. As women's social roles changed, they began to choose sportswear with shorter skirts with pleats, gathers, or slits, which permitted ease of motion. Low-waisted dresses with full hemlines allowed women to dance with ease to the new jazz music, while other styles, such as two-piece sweater and skirt outfits in luxurious wool jersey, were perfect for everyday wear.

The contents of A and L Tirocchi's shop were found in place in the house in 1989. This collection of textiles, costumes, and dressmaking records is now in the Rhode Island School of Design Museum of Art.

Tirocchi dress on loan from the Rhode Island School of Design Museum.

CONTRIBUTORS

Civil War Drum, courtesy of Varnum Memorial Armory.

Rhode Island Treasures thanks the following archives, museums and private collectors for their generosity in lending their treasures to the exhibition:

Barrington Preservation Society

Barrington Pavers

Black Heritage Society of Rhode Island

Sissieretta Jones' Dresses
Slave Shackles

Block Island Historical Society

Wrecking Cloth Quilt

Carousel Park Commission

Crescent Park Looff Dragon
Looff Carousel Horse
Glass Window from Looff Carousel

City of Warwick

Warwick City Charter
Mick Jagger Arrest Picture

East Providence Historical Society

Rumford Baking Powder Memorabilia
The New Crescent Park Poster

Shepard Fairey

Shepard Fairey *OBEY!* Stickers and Posters

Governor Henry Lippitt House Museum

Model of Governor Henry Lippitt House
Painting by Sydney Burleigh

Herreshoff Marine Museum

Herreshoff Steam Engine, 1893
Buzzards Bay 12^1/$_2$' Sailboat, 1928
Dubbed Video of America's Cup Race

John Hay Library, Brown University

Roger Williams, *Key Into the Language of America*, 1643
Roger Williams' Eliot Bible, 1663
Thomas Dorr's Personal Items in Prison
Elizabeth Buffum Chace Scrapbook
H.P. Lovecraft, *The Terrible Old Man* Manuscript
Pirates Poem
Sarah Whitman Portrait
Sarah Whitman Manuscript Letter
Rose Bowl Poster
Edgar Alan Poe, *To Helen*
Letter from Moses Brown
President Lincoln's Letter to Governors

Massasoit Historical Society

Scale Board from a Shipbuilder

Museum of Natural History at Roger Williams Park

RI Red Rooster
Cumberlandite Specimen
Bowenite Specimen

Naval Historical Collection, Naval War College

War of 1812 Manuscript Journal from Brig *Yankee*

Newport Historical Society

Newport Jazz Festival Commemorative Plate, 1958
Potter Family Painting, 1740

Pawtuxet Valley Preservation Society

World War I Uniform from a
    Rhode Island Soldier
Photograph of Rhode Island Soldier,
    Giacento Felix Lancellotta
Patches Worn by Apollo Astronauts
President Nixon Letter Regarding
    Apollo Patches

Pettaquanscutt Historical Society

Jonnycake Board

Preservation Society of Newport County

Construction Album of *The Breakers* Mansion,
    1894-1895
Bronze Portrait of Richard Morris Hunt, 1891

Providence Athenaeum

Edward Malbone Minuture Painting, *The Hours*
Edward Bannister Watercolors

Providence City Hall

Roger Williams and Narragansett Indian
    Land Deed, 1636

Providence Jewelry Museum

Butterfly Molds
Engraving Machine, 1910
Plating Machine Model, 1928
Wire Slitter, 1887
Stamping Press, 1870
Costume Jewelry
Rhinestones and Jewelers Tool

Providence Journal Company

Gorham Silver Tea Service

Providence Tourism Council

Treasures of Hope by Maxwell Mays

Redwood Library and Athenaeum

British Flag from Ship Bearing Rhode Island
    Royal Charter, 1663
Gilbert Stuart Self-Portrait, 1778
Townsend and Goddard Mahogany Table,
    1760-1775
Townsend and Goddard Furniture Book, 1754

Rhode Island College

Native American Clay Pots
Fishing and Hunting Tools
Silence by Nancy Prophet

Rhode Island Historical Society

Roger Williams Compass, 1650
Warwick Musical Theater T-Shirts
Independent Mr. Potato Head
Rhode Island Renunciation of Great Britain

Rhode Island Militia

Revolutionary War Backpack

Rhode Island School of Design Museum

Anna and Laura Tirocchi Dresses

Rhode Island State Archives

Bill of Rights
The People's Constitution, 1841
Battle of Aquidneck Island Map
Rhode Island Constitution
1784 Act Authorizing Manumission
    of Negroes, Mulattos and Others
Declaration of Independence
Gaspee Proclamation

Rhode Island State House

Nathanael Greene Sword

Ray Rickman (private collector)

Bill of Sale for a Slave

Slater Mill

Bevel Gear Mold
Replica of Carding Machine
Maypole Braider, 1872
Slater Mill Waterwheel Model

South County Museum

Victorian Hair Sculpture
Fog Horn
Sounding Lead
Hadley Quadrant, 1785
Azimuth Circle
1921 Model T Ford Depot Wagon
Slave Shackles
Slave Collar
Point Judith Lobster
Fishing Net
Shipwreck Map
Figurehead from Trading Vessel
    (courtesy of Mrs. Anita Hinckley)

The Society of Friends of Touro Synagogue

Scale Model of Touro Synagogue

University of Rhode Island

Head of *The Independent Man*

Varnum Memorial Armory

Revolutionary War Leather Helmet
Civil War Drum

Learn more about
Rhode Island and its
treasures from the
following resources:

BARRINGTON PRESERVATION SOCIETY
Box 178, 281 County Road   Barrington, RI 02806
401-247-3770

BLACK HERITAGE SOCIETY OF RHODE ISLAND
65 Weybossett Street, 2nd Floor, Suite 29   Providence, RI 02903
401-751-3490

BLOCK ISLAND HISTORICAL SOCIETY
P.O. Box 79   Block Island, RI 02807
401-466-2481

CAROUSEL PARK COMMISSION
147 Bell Avenue   Riverside, RI 02915
401-433-2466

EAST PROVIDENCE HISTORICAL SOCIETY
Hunts Mill Road, Box 4774   East Providence, RI 02916
401-438-1750   401-434-3347

FRIENDS OF LINDEN PLACE
500 Hope Street   Bristol, RI 02809
401-253-0390

GOVERNOR HENRY LIPPITT HOUSE MUSEUM
199 Hope Street   Providence, RI 02906
401-453-0688

HERITAGE HARBOR MUSEUM
222 Richmond Street   Providence, RI 02903
401-751-7979

HERRESHOFF MARINE MUSEUM
P.O. Box 450, 1 Burnside Street   Bristol, RI 02809
401-253-5000

THE JOHN HAY LIBRARY, BROWN UNIVERSITY
20 Prospect Street   Providence, RI 02912
401-863-2146

KENTISH GUARDS, RI MILITIA
1774 Armory Street   East Greenwich, RI 02818
401-739-8932

MASSASOIT HISTORICAL SOCIETY
17 Chase Avenue   Warren, RI 02885
401-245-1095

MUSEUM OF NATURAL HISTORY
Roger Williams Park   Providence, RI 02905
401-785-9457

NAVAL HISTORICAL COLLECTION, NAVAL WAR COLLEGE
686 Cushing Road   Newport, RI 02841
401-841-2435

NEWPORT HISTORICAL SOCIETY
82 Touro Street   Newport, RI 02840
401-846-0813

THE PRESERVATION SOCIETY OF NEWPORT COUNTY
424 Bellevue Avenue   Newport, RI 02840
401-847-1000

PAWTUXET VALLEY PRESERVATION SOCIETY
1679 Main Street   West Warwick, RI 02893
401-821-1078

PETTAQUAMSCUTT HISTORICAL SOCIETY
2636 Kingstown Road   Kingston, RI 02881
401-783-1328